WINE
APPRECIATION

Andrew Durkan and John Cousins

TEACH YOURSELF BOOKS

Long-renowned as the authoritative source for self-guided learning – with more than 30 million copies sold worldwide – the *Teach Yourself* series includes over 200 titles in the fields of languages, crafts, hobbies, sports, and other leisure activities.

British Library Cataloguing in Publication Data

A catalogue record for this title is available from the British Library

Library of Congress Catalog Card Number: 95-68141

First published in UK 1995 by Hodder Headline Plc, 338 Euston Road, London NW1 3BH

First published in US 1995 by NTC Publishing Group, 4255 West Touhy Avenue, Lincolnwood (Chicago), Illinois 60646 – 1975 U.S.A.

Typeset by Transet Ltd, Coventry, England.
Printed in England by Cox & Wyman Ltd, Reading, Berkshire.

Impression number	14	13	12	11	10	9	8	7	6	5	4	3	2
Year		1999		1998		1997		1996		1995			

CONTENTS

About the authors

Andrew Durkan

Andrew Durkan has over forty years' experience in the hotel and foodservice industry. He first developed an interest in wine through his association with the family hotel and bar business in the West of Ireland. After graduating from the Dublin Hotel School, he gained experience in both the United Kingdom and France, including working at London's Claridge's and Dorchester Hotels and the equally renowned Grand Hôtel de la Cloche in Dijon, France. He then held an Irish Government appointment as Inspector of Hotels.

After graduating from the University of London Teacher-Training Programme, he joined Ealing College where he became Senior Lecturer in Food and Beverage Operations. During his twenty-five years with the College (now part of Thames Valley University) he travelled extensively in the wine regions to further his knowledge and experience. He is a member of the Wine Society and in 1971 wrote the famous book *Vendange* which was the first text book on wines and alcoholic beverages. Since then he has contributed to a number of books including, together with John Cousins, *The Students' Guide to Food and Drink* and *The Beverage Book*, a new course book on wine and drinks.

Since retiring from full-time teaching, Andrew has continued to be a consultant to a major restaurant guide and a teacher for the Wine and Spirit Education Trust examinations. He also holds an appointment as Wine Lecturer and Consultant to The Savoy Group of Hotels and Restaurants and he has been honoured and intronised as Prud'Homme by La Jurade de Saint-Emilion.

John Cousins

John Cousins has thirty years' experience in the hotel and foodservice industry. After graduating from Stafford College and Birmingham College of Food, he entered the hotel industry and became an hotel manager at the age of twenty-four.

Having gained a variety of craft and management experience, he joined Ealing College (now part of Thames Valley University) where for the last fourteen years he has been a specialist in Food and Beverage Service Operations and Management. During this time he has developed his knowledge of wine and drink through research and travel and has gained postgraduate business and management qualifications, including a Henley MBA. He became a head of department in 1989 and since 1992 he has been the Head of The School of Hospitality Studies.

He is a Fellow of the Hotel and Catering International Management Association, the Cookery and Food Association and the Academy of Food and Wine Service. He is also a member of the Wine Society, an Académicien of the Académie Culinare de France and has been intronised as Prud'Homme by La Jurade de Saint-Emilion.

In addition to his authorship with Andrew Durkan he is the joint author, with Dennis Lillicrap, of the best-selling textbook *Food and Beverage Service*, now in its fourth edition. He currently holds the appointment as the United Kingdom waiting judge for the International Skill Olympics.

Acknowledgements

The authors would like to thank all those who have assisted in the preparation of this work and the provision of photographs. In particular: The Champagne Information Bureau; Food and Wine from France; The German Wine Information Service; Gonzales Byass; The Italian Trade Centre; The Sherry Institute.

Additional thanks to Janet Price, Joe Douglas, Heinz Jaron, Clay Leitch.

FOREWORD

If you have tasted wine and you like it, then this book is intended to help you develop your interest further. Wine is a source of pleasure and of lasting interest. Learning about wine is as much about gaining experience as it is about gaining knowledge. Indeed the learning is the experience. It is about sensation, feeling, the occasion, the accompanying food and the company, as well as about memory. It is also a never-ending source of fascination. Wine appreciation is the experience of all these things. Learning about wine requires a combination of the experience gained through the use of the senses and the use of the brain which records the sensation.

First, though, it is worth remembering that we are all different, particularly in our ability to taste. The palate is not fixed; it develops with age and all of us are somewhere on the journey. This is one of the reasons why our tastes change. When we are young we tend to prefer sweeter drinks, but as we mature we begin to move towards drier drinks, then we learn to appreciate more subtle or sophisticated flavours. But there is no guarantee that any of us will be at a particular point at a certain time. Some people will always prefer milder and less dry drinks: others will find that their tastes change at different times. Therefore, always be confident in buying and enjoying the wine *you* like and always trust your own judgement.

Wine appreciation

For the appreciation of wine there are some key skills and some knowledge to be mastered. This will help to provide you with a framework to which you can relate your existing and future experience of wine. It also helps to provide a guide to the world of wine and your exploration of it. The two key skills in wine appreciation are reading the label and tasting. The label is the wine's birth certificate and it provides information about the wine. The tasting provides the sensation of the wine. This book is intended to support you in developing your ability to read and understand the label and to register colour, smell and the sensation of taste. Most of all it is intended to encourage you in your enjoyment of wine.

Chapter 1 describes how and where wine is made, the styles that are available, the grapes that are used, and identifies some of the faults that can occur in wine. It also explains the best way to serve wine.

Chapter 2 discusses how we taste wine, suggests a tasting procedure and also reminds us that wine is alcohol. Some advice on sensible drinking is, therefore, also given.

Chapter 3 provides advice on the buying of wine in the restaurant and for the home. A section on ideal conditions for storage will help you to keep your wine at its most drinkable.

Chapter 4 gives guidelines on the matching of wine and food. It offers good combinations and suggests the best wines to complement sample menus.

In Chapter 5 there is a detailed A to Z listing of the wine-growing regions of the world. Information is given on the region, the wines that are produced and the language of labels.

Wine-based drinks, brandy and aromatised wines and bitters are dealt with in Chapter 6. A selection of wine-based mixed drinks is also detailed.

At the end of the book you will find some questions you may like answered, a glossary, suggestions for further reading and a comprehensive index.

How to use this book

We suggest that you read Chapter 1 – Introduction to wine –

first. This provides the basic knowledge about what wine is and how it varies. It also introduces some key wine terms, relating to production techniques, viticulture, grape varieties and styles of wine.

Then move on to tasting wine, Chapter 2, which should be accompanied by some practice! This will help you to develop a frame of reference for remembering tasting experiences. We also suggest that you begin to compile your own record of experience based on the factors you have identified.

After that it really is up to you, but some approaches are:

Following grape varieties

If you find that you particularly like a wine made from a certain grape such as Chardonnay, then try wines from different parts of the world made from the same variety. This will expose you to the variation in wines which are a result of location and local tradition.

Following styles

If you have a preference for, say, dry whites, then try these from different regions and from different grape varieties. This will help you to identify the characteristics of individual wines. It will also help you to develop your knowledge of which variety of grape gives the best result in each style of wine.

Following countries

If you find that you especially like wines from, say, Italy, then explore the various wines produced by that country. This will provide the opportunity to develop your knowledge of a particular country as well as determining your preferences for individual styles of wine and grape varieties.

Following regions

Where you prefer a wine from a particular region or district, such as Saint-Emilion in Bordeaux, explore the range of wines available from that region to increase your knowledge of it, as well as the differences between young and old wines and the various classes of wine.

Linking with food

One way of increasing your understanding and appreciation of food and wine combinations is to plan to try different wines with a range of foods. This will help you to identify how taste sensation can be affected by each wine that you use with a certain dish. Alternatively, you could try a combination of a variety of foods with the same wine.

Whichever approach you decide to follow, whether it is one of the above or a combination of them, we suggest that you plan your reading to coincide with the tasting experience. This will help to reinforce the sensation and will also, over time, increase your knowledge and your ability to select or recommend wines.

Above all enjoy the journey and always accept that sometimes you might get it wrong and sometimes the experience will be exquisite: this is the fun and joy of discovery. The unpredictability of wine is part of its fascination.

1
INTRODUCTION TO WINE

Wine making

Wine is as old as history. The spread of the vine started with the Assyrians and was carried on by the Phoenicians, the Greeks, Romans and religious orders. Later, it was continued by exiles such as the Italians, Germans, Spanish and French who established vineyards wherever they formed into large communities in areas compatible with the cultivation of the vine.

Fig. 1.1 A typical wine-producing landscape (Alsace)

Wine is fermented grape juice, the best quality being produced mostly in the latitudes 30–50° north and south of the Equator. There are four main families of wine-producing vines: *Vitis vinifera* (wine bearing) which produces all the great wines, and *Vitis riparia*, *Vitis labrusca* and *Vitis rupestris* which make less-fine wines.

Wine making has never been easy, and wine growers down the ages have had to contend with and protect their vines from all kinds of pests and diseases such as oidium, mildew, grey rot, cochylis, rougeot, chlorose, coulure and browning. The worst pest of all was the dreadful *Phylloxera vastatrix*. This aphid, which lives in a gall on the under-side of the vine leaf, or on the roots, was brought from North America to Europe in the latter half of the nineteenth century. It attacked the vine roots and devastated most of the world's vineyards. Later on it was discovered that American rootstocks (e.g. *Vitis rupestris*) were resistant to the disease. Thus, today most vines are grafted on to American stocks.

The grape

The grape, which has developed on the vine for about 100 days after flowering, is made up of skin, stalk, pips and pulp.

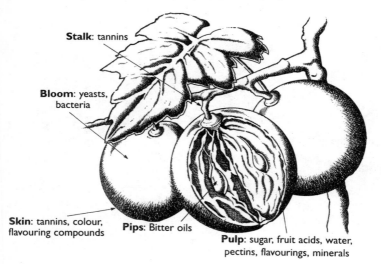

Stalk: tannins

Bloom: yeasts, bacteria

Skin: tannins, colour, flavouring compounds

Pips: Bitter oils

Pulp: sugar, fruit acids, water, pectins, flavourings, minerals

Fig. 1.2 The wine-producing properties of the grape

Skin

The outer skin (cuticle) is coated with a waxy film (bloom) on which there are, by the time the grape is ripe, about 100,000 wine yeasts plus 10 million wild yeasts and other micro-organisms. Wine yeasts (*Saccharomyces ellipsoideus*) spend winter in the intestines of animals and in spring they are disseminated to alight on flowers and plants. In summer the wind and insects carry them to settle on the ripening grape skins where they are trapped by the waxy film and form a downy coating on the grape. Each yeast contains thousands of minute enzymes (ferments). When these come in contact with the sugars in the grape juice and air, a chemical reaction, known as fermentation, takes place.

The inside of the grape skin contains colouring matter which is extracted during fermentation by the alcohol.

Fig. 1.3 Wine fermenting

Stalks

When used in wine making (red wine in particular), the stalks provide tannic acid which gives body and keeping qualities to wine. If over used, this acid can cause wine to become too astringent and nasty. However, when used correctly it gives wine a dry flavour and a good grip on the palate. During the maturing process of wine, tannic acid helps to coagulate the fining agent as the wine is being clarified.

Pips

The pips, if crushed, impart tannic acid and oils to the wine.

Pulp

The pulp provides the grape juice or must and contains:

- 78–80 per cent   water
- 10–25 per cent   sugar
- 5–6 per cent   acids

Water
Water makes up the bulk of wine.

Sugar
Sugar is formed in the grapes by sunlight and is of two kinds, grape sugar (dextrose and glucose) and fruit sugar (levulose and fructose). It is found in about equal quantities in the must and is essential to the fermenting process.

Fig. 1.4 Cooling coils in a barrel, used to slow down fermentation

Acids
Tartaric, malic, tannic and citric acids help to give keeping quality, freshness, brilliance and balance. When they come in contact with alcohol, esters are formed and it is these that give a wine its bouquet.

The must (unfermented grape juice) will also have trace elements of nitrogenous compounds such as albumen, peptones, amides, ammonium salts and nitrates, as well as potassium, phosphoric acid and calcium, all of which have an influence on the eventual taste of the wine.

How wine is made

The making of wine starts with the gathering of the grapes (the vintage). The grapes are crushed to produce the must. This is run off into huge temperature-controlled vats where fermentation takes place. Fermentation, which can last from a week to three weeks, is the action of yeast (found on the bloom covering the outside skin of the grape) on the sugar in the must, converting it into ethyl alcohol and carbon dioxide gas (CO_2) through a series of complex biochemical reactions. The gas forms bubbles on the surface before escaping into the air.

There are two types of yeast: wild yeasts which start the fermentation and are killed when the alcohol level reaches 4 per cent by volume and wine yeasts which then take over and can continue to convert the sugar up to a maximum of 16 per cent alcohol by volume. Most table wines however, have an alcohol strength of between 10 per cent and 14 per cent.

The new wine is usually transferred to casks where it will be racked from time to time as it matures. The purpose of racking is to eliminate the lees (sediment or deposit) in the wine. This deposit is left behind as the wine is moved to a fresh cask and so, with each racking, the wine becomes clearer. Before being bottled the wine is fined to get rid of unwanted particles held in suspension. Isinglass, egg whites, gelatine and dried albumen are particularly good fining agents as they attract the unwanted particles and drag them down to the bottom of the cask, thus leaving behind brilliant wine which may or may

---

not be filtered before bottling. The longer the wine matures in cask the less time it needs in bottle. Great wines are matured for many years in bottle.

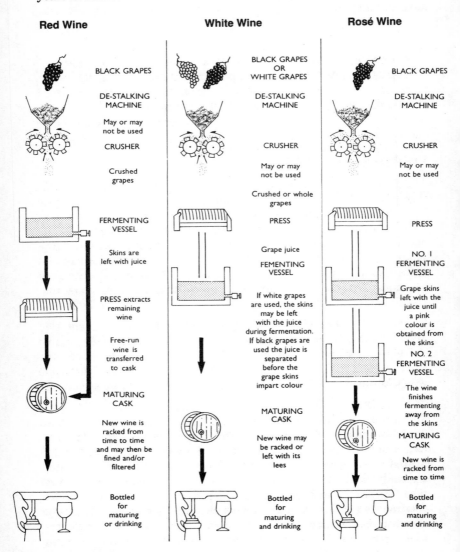

Red Wine

BLACK GRAPES

DE-STALKING MACHINE

May or may not be used

CRUSHER

Crushed grapes

FERMENTING VESSEL

Skins are left with juice

PRESS extracts remaining wine

Free-run wine is transferred to cask

MATURING CASK

New wine is racked from time to time and may then be fined and/or filtered

Bottled for maturing or drinking

White Wine

BLACK GRAPES OR WHITE GRAPES

DE-STALKING MACHINE

CRUSHER

May or may not be used

Crushed or whole grapes

PRESS

Grape juice

FEMENTING VESSEL

If white grapes are used, the skins may be left with the juice during fermentation. If black grapes are used the juice is separated before the grape skins impart colour

MATURING CASK

New wine may be racked or left with its lees

Bottled for maturing and drinking

Rosé Wine

BLACK GRAPES

DE-STALKING MACHINE

CRUSHER

May or may not be used

PRESS

NO. 1 FERMENTING VESSEL

Grape skins left with the juice until a pink colour is obtained from the skins

NO. 2 FERMENTING VESSEL

The wine finishes fermenting away from the skins

MATURING CASK

New wine is racked from time to time

Bottled for maturing and drinking

Fig. 1.5 How wine is made

Factors that influence the quality of wine

Several factors influence the quality of wine. These are soil, climate, microclimate, aspect, terroir, grape variety, viticulture, vinification and the luck of the year.

Soil

Vineyards usually thrive where other crops struggle. Poor soils rich in minerals are best for the vine as they provide nutrients such as phosphate, iron, potassium, magnesium and calcium – all of which contribute to the final taste of the wine. Favoured soils are chalk, limestone, slate, sand, schist, gravel, pebbles, clay, aluvial and volcanic. These soils have good drainage and moisture retention to keep the vine roots healthy. Drainage is especially important, as the vine does not like to have wet feet. Soil is analysed annually and any chemical deficiency is compensated for.

Climate

The vine needs a good balance of moisture and heat. Temperature is ideally continental averaging 14–16°C (57–61°F). The lowest annual average temperature necessary for the vine to flourish is 10°C (50°F). It is estimated that the vine needs about 69 cm (26 inches) of rain per year – mainly in winter and spring – and at least 1,400 hours of sunshine per year. A prolonged growing season allows the grape to develop and ripen slowly, resulting in more definite aromas and more pronounced fruit flavours.

Microclimate

This particular and usually beneficial climate prevails in a single vineyard or a group of vineyards or within a small region. It could be caused by hills or mountains protecting the vines from heavy winds or even a break in the mountain range allowing the air to freshen and fan the vines in very hot weather. Sometimes the angle of the sun, especially the clear brilliant morning sun, will strike one vineyard more favourably than another. The rise and fall of the terrain will also have an effect as will location beside water for moisture and reflected heat. These subtle differences in atmospheric conditions, allied to the quality of the soil and the grape variety used, are the reason why some vineyards have such outstanding reputations.

Aspect

Vineyards are ideally planted on south-facing slopes where they point towards the sun and benefit from maximum sunshine and good drainage. Siting is of prime importance to capture the sunlight for photosynthesis and good ripening. Some vineyards are sited as high as 240 m (800 ft) or more on mountainsides, while many of the great vineyards are located in river valleys and by the side of lakes benefiting from humidity and reflected heat.

Terroir

This incorporates the combined effects of soil and subsoil, climate, location (including aspect and altitude) and microclimate; in other words the complete growing environment of the vine.

Grape variety

The grape must be in harmony with the soil, the location of the vineyard and local climatic conditions. It must also be reasonably disease resistant, give a good yield and produce the best quality wine possible. Wine is produced from either varietal grapes – usually a classic single grape like the Riesling or from hybrids which are a cross, for example: Riesling x Silvaner = Müller-Thurgau. Grapes behave differently in different soils: for example, Pinot Noir is a classic in Burgundy and a disaster in Bordeaux. Older vines yield superior quality grapes, although the yield is less abundant.

Viticulture

This is the cultivation of the vine. An overworked vineyard without compensatory treatment, or a neglected vineyard, will produce only second-rate wine. So the farming of the vineyard is of prime importance. It deals with:

● vine selection
● keeping the vineyard healthy
● ploughing to aerate the soil
● weeding
● fertilising
● pruning to regulate quality (pruning restricts the yield and improves grape quality)

- training the vines
- spraying to combat diseases
- harvesting

Vinification

Vinification is the making of the wine which encompasses:

- pressing the grapes
- the treatment and fermentation of the must
- maturing the wine and occasionally topping it up to keep the air out
- racking, fining and filtration to make the wine star-bright
- blending – compensatory or otherwise
- bottling for further maturing or for sale

Luck of the year

In some years, everything in the vineyards and cellars combines well to produce a wine of excellence – a vintage wine. In other years, there can be great disappointments brought on by an excess of climatic conditions: sun, rain, snow, frost and the dreaded hail, which will produce either poor wine or worse. So the wine grower can never be confident, but must always be vigilant.

THE WINE YEAR IN THE NORTHERN HEMISPHERE

January   Starts with pruning the vines and general maintenance to walls, posts and the wire used for vine training.

February   Pruning, to regulate quality, continues and cuttings are taken for grafting. Machinery is cleaned, oiled and put in good working order.

March   Pruning is completed and ploughing begins to aerate the soil. This allows roots to breathe and facilitates free drainage of water to the roots. Bench grafting takes place.

April   Ploughing is completed, weeding continues and year-old cuttings are planted out.

May   Vines are treated with copper sulphate against mildew, Vine suckers are removed.

June   The vines flower and treatment (spraying) continues.

July   Weeding and spraying continues. Overlong green shoots are pinched back.

August   Weeding, as before, and trimming of the vines to allow maximum sunshine to the grape bunches. Wine-making apparatus is prepared. Grapes swell and begin to change colour.

September Grapes continue to swell and colour deepens. White grapes change to yellow-green. Black grapes change from yellow-green to violet or deep purple. Sunshine is badly needed now to finish the ripening. Refractometers are taken into the vineyards to gauge the sugar level within the grapes. That, and the acidity level, will decide when the vintage can begin. Traditionally the grapes should be perfectly ripe and ready 100 days after flowering. Bands of pickers will be contracted and the vintage usually starts about the third week in September, depending on location.

October   The cellarmaster finishes making the wine. Fermentation can take from six days to six weeks depending on the style of wine. Vineyards are deep ploughed and fertilised with chemicals to compensate for any deficiencies.

November More fertilising. Long shoots are cut off and the base of the vines are 'hilled up' with soil for protection against snow and frost.

December Wine equipment is cleaned and stored away. Deep ploughing of soil continues. Minor pruning commences and the cycle of work starts once more.

The top ten wine-producing countries by volume

1	Italy	6	CIS (formerly USSR)
2	France	7	Portugal
3	Spain	8	Germany
4	Argentina	9	Romania
5	USA	10	South Africa

This order is according to the volume of wine produced and it has been known to change periodically.

Wine styles

Red wine

Red wine comes from black grapes that are fermented throughout with their skins and sometimes also with their stalks. As fermentation continues the alcohol generated draws colour from the inside of the skins.

Rosé wine

Rosé wine comes from black grapes without the stalks and is made in a similar way to red wine, but the juice is separated once the desired degree of pinkness has been achieved. Fermentation is completed in a separate vessel. Alternative methods are either to press the grapes so that some colour is extracted from the skins or to blend red and white wine together.

Blush wine

Blush wine is a new style of rosé wine originating in California in which the black grape skins are left to macerate for only a very short period with the must. The resulting wine has a blue-pink hue with copper highlights.

White wine

White wine comes from either black or white grapes. When black grapes are used, the juice is quickly moved to another vessel to begin and complete its fermentation. All grape juice is colourless initially. The juice from white grapes is usually left with the grape skins until fermentation is completed.

Sparkling wine

When making sparkling wine, a sugar solution and special yeast culture are added first to dry table wine. The wine is then sealed and a secondary fermentation is allowed to take place:

- in a bottle (*méthode Champenoise* or *méthode traditionnelle*)
- in a tank (*méthode cuve close* – also known as the Charmat or bulk method)
- in a bottle and then the wine is transferred under pressure to a tank or vat where it is filtered and rebottled (*méthode transvasement* – transfer method)

Sparkling wine can also be made by injecting CO_2 into the chilled vats of still wine and then bottling the wine under pressure (*méthode gazifié*) also known in France as *méthode pompe bicyclette*.

Organic wines

These wines, also known as 'green' or 'environmentally friendly' wines, are made from grapes grown without the aid of artificial insecticides, pesticides or fertiliser. The wine itself will not be adulterated in any way, save for minimal amounts of the traditional preservative, sulphur dioxide, which is controlled at source.

Alcohol-free, de-alcoholised wines and low alcohol wines

- alcohol-free   maximum   0.05 per cent alcohol
- de-alcoholised   maximum   0.50 per cent alcohol
- low alcohol   maximum   1.25 per cent alcohol

Leaving aside the commercial angle, these wines have been produced as a response to today's emphasis on health and fitness. Specifically, they are aimed at the designated driver, the weight watcher, the medical patient, the sports enthusiast, the business man, those on diets with a restricted alcohol intake and even at the non-drinker. The wines are made in the normal way and the alcohol is then removed either by the hot treatment, distillation, which unfortunately removes most of the flavour as well, or, more satisfactorily, by the cold filtration process, also known as reverse osmosis. This removes the alcohol by mechanically separating or filtering out the molecules of alcohol through membranes made of cellulose of acetate. The wine is repeatedly passed through the membranes which filter out the alcohol and water, leaving behind a syrupy wine concentrate. To this, at a later stage, water and a little must are added, thus preserving much of the flavour or mouthfeel of the original wine.

Vins doux naturels

These are sweet wines that have had their fermentation muted by the addition of alcohol in order to retain their natural sweetness. Muting takes place when the alcohol level reaches between 5 per cent and 8 per cent by volume. They have a final alcoholic strength of about 17 per cent by volume. A well known example is Muscat de Beaumes-de-Venise (see page 95).

Fortified wines

Fortified wines such as sherry (pages 131–135), port (pages 126–128) and Madeira (pages 128–129) are those that have been strengthened by the addition of alcohol, usually a grape spirit.

Aromatised wines

These are flavoured and usually fortified. Typical examples are vermouths (page 157) and Commandaria (page 65).

--------- # Grapes for wine ---------

The following is a list of the principal grapes used in wine production in the main wine-growing regions of the world.

Fig. 1.6 Chardonnay grapes

Fig. 1.7 Palomino grapes

White grapes

Aligoté	Burgundy
Bacchus	mainly Germany but also grown in England
Blanc Fumé	*see* Sauvignon Blanc
Blanquette	*see* Columbard
Bual (Boal)	Madeira
Catawba	North American states (*Vitis labrusca*)
Chardonnay	Champagne, Burgundy, California, Eastern Europe, South America, Australia and New Zealand; sometimes referred to as Pinot Chardonnay
Chasselas	France – mainly the Loire (e.g. Pouilly-sur-Loire); Central Europe; known as Gutedel in Germany and Fendant in Switzerland

Chauche Gris	*see* Grey Riesling
Chenin Blanc	Loire (e.g. Vouvray, Saumur, Coteaux du Layon), California, South America, South Africa (known as Steen), Australia
Clairette	mainly southern France
Colombard	France, especially in Cognac (also known as Blanquette elsewhere in France), California (known as French Colombard)
Delaware	North America states (*Vitis labrusca*)
Fendant	*see* Chasselas
Folle Blanche	France, especially Cognac, Armagnac and the Loire, and California; also known as Picpoule
French Colombard	*see* Colombard
Furmint	Hungary (e.g. Tokay); also known as Sipon in Hungary
Gewürztraminer	France – in Alsace (also in the Jura where it is known as Savagnin); Germany, Austria, Australia, northern Italy, California
Grey Riesling	France, California; real name Chauche Gris
Gutedel	*see* Chasselas
Johannisberg Riesling	Germany – mainly Rhine and Mosel; France – in Alsace and the Jura; Central Europe, Australia, California; also called White Riesling
Listan Palomino	*see* Palomino
Malmsey	*see* Malvasia
Malvasia	California, Mediterranean; known as Malmsey in Madeira
Malvoisie	*see* Pinot Gris
Melon de Bourgogne	France – in Muscadet; also known as Muscadet
Müller-Thurgau	England, Germany, Austria, Central Europe
Muscadelle	mainly in Australia, South Africa and some in France (in Bordeaux)

Muscadet	*see* Melon de Bourgogne
Muscat	France (e.g. Muscat de Beaumes-de-Venise), California, Spain, Italy (e.g. Asti Spumante), Mediterranean
Palomino	Spain for sherry; also known as Listan Palomino
Pedro Ximénez	Australia, California, South Africa, Spain for sherry
Picpoule	*see* Folle Blanche
Pinot Blanc	Burgundy, Alsace, Germany (where it is known as Weissburgunder), Italy, California
Pinot Chardonnay	*see* Chardonnay
Pinot Grigio	*see* Pinot Gris
Pinot Gris	France – mainly Alsace; Germany, Switzerland, northern Italy; known as Pinot Grigio in Italy, Ruländer in Germany, Tokay in Alsace and Malvoisie in Switzerland
Riesling	*see* Johannisberg Riesling and Sémillion
Ruländer	*see* Pinot Gris
Saint-Emilion	*see* Ugni Blanc
Savagnin	*see* Gewürztraminer
Sauvignon Blanc	France – mainly Loire Valley (e.g. Sancerre and Pouilly Fumé) and

Fig. 1.8 Sylvaner grapes

Fig. 1.9 Grenache grapes

	Bordeaux (e.g. Graves and Sauternes); Chile, Australia, California; also called Blanc Fumé
Sémillon	France – mainly Bordeaux (e.g. Graves and Sauternes); South America, South Africa, Australia, California; often called Riesling in Australia
Sercial	Madeira
Seyval Blanc	North American states, Canada, France, England
Silvaner	*see* Sylvaner
Sipon	*see* Furmint
Steen	*see* Chenin Blanc
Sylvaner	Central Europe – mainly Germany; France – in Alsace; California; also known as Silvaner
Tokay	*see* Pinot Gris
Trebbiano	Italy (e.g. Soave, Orvieto, Frascati), France, California; also known as Ugni Blanc
Ugni Blanc	France mainly Cognac and Armagnac where it is known as Saint-Emilion; also *see* Trebbiano
Verdelho	Madeira
Verdicchio	mainly central Italy
Viognier	France mainly Rhône (e.g. Condrieu)
Welschriesling	Europe; no relation to Johannisberg Riesling
Weissburgunder	*see* Pinot Blanc
White Riesling	*see* Johannisberg Riesling

Red grapes

Baco Noir	North American states, France
Barbera	Italy – in Piedmont; South America, California
Bouchet	*see* Cabernet Franc
Brunello	Italy – in Tuscany (e.g. Brunello di Montalcino)

Cabernet Franc	France – mainly Loire (e.g. Cabernet d'Anjou, Chinon) and Bordeaux; Italy, California; also known as Bouchet in France
Cabernet Sauvignon	France – mainly Bordeaux and Provence; Chile, Bulgaria, California, Spain, Australia, almost everywhere
Carignan	France – mainly Rhône and Provence; California, Spain, North Africa
Chancellor Noir	North American states, southern France
Charbono	California
Cinsault	France
Concorde	North American states, California (*Vitis labrusca*)
de Chaunac	North American states, Canada
Dolcetto	Italy – in Piedmont
Duriff	*see* Petit Sirah
Gamay	France – mainly Beaujolais but also Loire; Switzerland, California
Gamay Beaujolais	California
Grenache	France – mainly south and southern Rhône (e.g. Châteauneuf-du-Pape, with other grapes, and for Tavel Rosé and Lirac), California, Spain
Lambrusco	Italy – in Emilia-Romagna
Malbec	France – in Bordeaux; Cahors, Argentina, California
Merlot	France – mainly Bordeaux; northern Italy, Switzerland, California, South America, South Africa
Meunier	France – in Champagne; also called Pinot Meunier
Nebbiolo	Italy – in Piedmont and Lombardy (e.g. Barolo, Barbaresco); California
Petit Sirah	California; also called Duriff
Pinot Meunier	*see* Meunier
Pinot Noir	France – mainly Champagne and Burgundy, but also in the Loire; England, Switzerland, Germany (known as Spätburgunder), Eastern Europe,

Pinotage	California, South America (Pinot Noir/Cinsault cross) South Africa, New Zealand

Fig. 1.10 Merlot grapes   **Fig. 1.11** Zinfandel grapes

Ruby Cabernet	California
Sangiovese	Italy – in Tuscany and Emilia-Romagna (e.g. for Chianti, but blended with other grapes)
Shiraz	*see* Syrah
Spätburgunder	*see* Pinot Noir
Syrah	France – mainly northern Rhône (e.g. Hermitage, St Joseph, Cornas, also used in blend for Châteauneuf-du-Pape); Australia; also known as Shiraz
Tempranillo	Spain – Rioja; Argentina
Zinfandel	California; also used for blush and rosé wines

———— Faults in wine ————

Faults occasionally develop in wine as it matures in bottle. Nowadays, through improved technique and attention to detail regarding bottling and storage, faulty wine is a rarity. However,

—

occasionally you may be unfortunate enough to come across a rogue bottle. Here are the more common causes.

Corked wines

These are wines affected by a diseased cork caused through bacterial action or excessive bottle age. The wine tastes and smells foul. Not to be confused with cork residue in wine which is harmless.

Maderisation or oxidation

This is caused by bad storage: too much exposure to air, often because the cork has dried out in these conditions. The colour of the wine browns or darkens and the taste very slightly resembles Madeira, hence the name. The wine tastes 'spoilt'.

Acetification

Acetification is caused when the wine is overexposed to air. The vinegar micro-organism develops a film on the surface of the wine and acetic acid is produced making the wine taste sour resembling wine vinegar (*vin aigre*).

Tartrate flake

This is the crystallisation of potassium bitartrate. These crystal-like flakes, sometimes seen in white wine, may cause anxiety to some customers as they spoil the appearance of the wine which is otherwise perfect to drink. If the wine is stabilised before bottling, this condition should not occur.

Excess sulphur dioxide (SO$_2$)

Sulphur dioxide is added to wine to preserve it and keep it healthy. Once the bottle is opened the stink will disappear and, after a few minutes, the wine is perfectly drinkable.

Secondary fermentation

This happens when traces of sugar and yeast are left in the wine in bottle. It leaves the wine with an unpleasant, prickly taste that should not be confused with the *pétillant*, *spritzig* characteristics associated with other styles of healthy and refreshing wines.

Foreign contamination

Examples include splintered or powdered glass caused by faulty bottling machinery or re-used bottles which previously held some kind of disinfectant.

Hydrogen sulphide (H₂S)

The wine has the characteristic smell of rotten eggs. Throw it away.

Sediment, lees, crust or dregs

This comprises organic matter discarded by the wine as it matures in cask or bottle. It can be removed by racking, fining or, in the case of bottled wine, by decanting.

Cloudiness

This is caused by suspended matter in the wine disguising its true colour. It may be due to extremes in storage temperatures.

——————— The service of wine ———————

Whether at home or in a restaurant, one of the main concerns of any host is to have the wine to be offered to the guests properly temperatured. This is a basic requirement and gives the wine a real chance to shine. Ideally, one should know the food on offer so that a wine can be organised in advance and the appropriate temperature assured.

Opening techniques

First, cut away the top of the capsule to expose the cork. Above all, use a corkscrew with a wide thread so that the cork can be levered out without any crumbling. The cork should leave the bottle with a sigh as if sad to depart after such long contact. Smell the cork which should smell of wine. Sometimes a wine may have a bit of bottle stink due to stale air being lodged between cork and wine, but this soon disappears as the wine is exposed to air.

Red wine bottles are usually placed on a coaster beside the host, whereas sparkling, white, blush and rosé bottles should be placed in a wine bucket holding ice and water up to the neck of the bottle. In a restaurant it is very important to show the host the bottle with the label uppermost and to nominate the wine verbally so there is no confusion regarding the wine or vintage ordered.

Pour, twist and take

When pouring wine, the neck of the bottle should be over the glass, but not resting on the rim in case of an accident. Care should be taken to avoid splashing and, having finished pouring, the bottle should be twisted as it is being taken away. This will prevent drips of wine falling on the tablecloth or on someone's clothes. Any drops on the rim of the bottle should be taken away with a clean service cloth or napkin.

The host gets a little taster and decides that the wine is perfectly sound for drinking. Service proceeds on the right from the right around the table with the label clearly visible and with the host's glass being finally topped-up to the customary two-thirds full. Later, if another bottle of the same is ordered, the host should be given a fresh glass from which to taste the new wine.

Opening and serving Champagne and sparkling wines

Champagne and sparkling wines can be a bit of a problem. The bottle should not be shaken on its journey to the table and the wine must be well chilled. This helps control the effervescence and imparts the refreshing qualities associated with such wines.

Loosen or take off the wire muzzle. Holding the bottle at an angle of 45° in one hand and the cork in the other, twist the bottle *only* and, when the cork begins to move, restrain it by pushing it almost back into the neck. Soon the cork will leave the bottle quietly (never with a loud pop or bang). Should the cork prove stubborn and reluctant to leave the bottle, soak a napkin in hot water, wrap it around the neck of the bottle and movement will occur quickly.

Be extra careful when opening sparkling wines. Always keep the palm of your hand over the cork to prevent accidents to the eyes and elsewhere. Hold the bottle with your thumb in the punt and pour the wine against the inside of the glass – there should be a nice mousse but no frothing over.

Fig. 1.12 Sparkling, red, rosé and white wine in appropriate glasses

Decanting

The main reasons for decanting an old red wine are (a) to separate it from the sediment, (b) to allow the wine to breathe and (c) to develop its bouquet. Fine old red wines and some ports which have spent most of their lives maturing in bottle throw a deposit or crust which, if allowed to enter the glass, would sully the appearance of the wine. This deposit forms as the wine ages and consists of tannins, bitartrates of calcium and magnesium and colouring matter. It makes the wine cloudy and can cause it to taste of lees.

Decanting is the movement of wine from its original container to a fresh glass receptacle, leaving the gunge or sediment behind. It is best to stand the bottle upright for two days before decanting to give the sediment a chance to settle at the bottom.

1 Extract the cork carefully – it may disintegrate because of long contact with alcohol, so be wary;
2 Place a light behind the shoulder of the bottle, a candle if you are decanting in front of guests, but a torch, light bulb or any light

source at home or in the cellar will do;

3   Carefully pour the wine through a funnel into an absolutely clean decanter. The light will reveal the first sign of sediment (known as beeswing in port) entering the neck of the bottle;

4   At this stage stop pouring into the decanter but continue pouring into a glass which should be handy. The latter wine when it settles can be used as a taster or for sauces in the kitchen and can provide a nice talking point for guests.

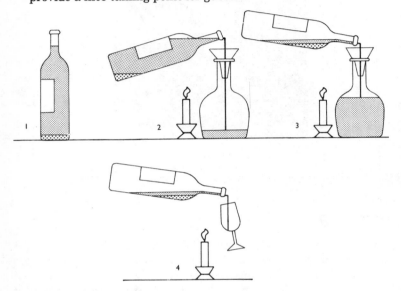

Fig. 1.13 Decanting wine

The quick method for decanting is to place a coffee filter or perfectly clean muslin in a funnel which should be in the neck of the decanter as the wine flows in. The vogue nowadays is also to decant younger red wines, simply because exposure to air improves the bouquet, and softens and mellows the wine. Of course, the host's permission must always be given before decanting a wine in a restaurant. Decanting also enhances the appearance of the wine, especially when presented in a fine wine decanter.

At home, experiment by pouring young and robust red wine into glasses 15 minutes before the meal – not only will the wine taste smoother, but the room will be pleasingly redolent of wine as the guests enter.

Very old red wine breaks up with too much exposure to air. It is best to stand such a bottle for a few days to allow the sediment to settle in the bottom. Then open the bottle just before the meal is served and pour the wine very carefully straight into the glass with the bottle held in the pouring position as each glass is approached. This prevents the wine slopping back to disturb the sediment. Sufficient glasses should be available to finish the bottle, thereby ensuring that the wine does not remingle with its sediment at the end of service.

Wine cradles or wine baskets are useful when taking old red wines from the cellar as they hold the bottle in the binned position, thus leaving the sediment undisturbed. If great care is taken when pouring, you can avoid disturbing the sediment by using the cradle, but the skill requires expertise and a large hand to span the cradle. It has become fashionable to serve red wines in a wine basket. While this practice appeals to some, there is no technical argument for doing so.

Carafe wines, also known as house wines, should be pleasant to drink and may be red, white or rosé. Just as the quality of soup tells you about the chef's approach to cooking, so the house wine reveals the restaurant's attitude to wine. Unlike the decanter, which is often made of cut glass and has a stopper fitted, a carafe is usually plain, of clear glass and without a stopper.

RECOMMENDED SERVICE TEMPERATURES

Champagne and sparkling wines (red, white, rosé)	4.5–7°C (40–45°F)
Sweet white wines	7–10°C (45–50°F)
White and rosé wines	10–12.5°C (50–55°F)
Young light red wines	12.5–15.5°C (55–60°F)
Full-bodied red wines	15.5–18°C (60–65°F)

Desperate situations, desperate remedies

When guests call unexpectedly you can chill wines quickly by placing a bottle in a wine bucket containing, salt, ice and water. The salt quickly melts the ice and drastically reduces the temperature. Another way is to place the wine in the freezer for about 10 minutes. A cool red wine can be brought to room temperature by being poured into a warmed decanter or by microwaving it for about 45 seconds.

Remember these are *extreme* situations – nothing beats traditional methods of chilling and chambréing wine to a perfect temperature. With wine, perfection is not everything, it is the *only* thing – it takes time.

How to prevent wasting wine

Wine that is left over in a bottle, even when securely corked, becomes lifeless and unpalatable after a couple of days, so down the drain it goes. To prevent this waste, a neat piece of equipment exists called a *Vacu-vin* which will reseal an opened bottle of wine, keeping the contents in perfect condition for several days. It extracts the air from the bottle and then reseals it with a special reuseable stopper that preserves the natural freshness of the wine for a longer period, allowing you to drink as much as you like, when you like. There is also a sparkling wine bottle resealer which is particularly useful for Champagne and other bottles of fizz.

2

WINE TASTING

Tasting procedures

A more apt name for wine tasting is sensory evaluation because sight, smell and touch are also involved in the process of appraisal, acceptance or rejection. It is estimated that taste may be at least 80 per cent smell. As proof, try tasting when you have a heavy cold. We taste mainly to savour the product, to assess quality and relate it to price. We also taste to check and record the drink's condition, to monitor progress and to determine its potential. Ideally, serious tasting should be done in perfect conditions such as:

- good natural daylight
- in a room with north-facing windows where the light is not subject to variations
- where there is no possibility of competing with distracting, pungent odours
- where conditions are comfortable and where there is sufficient space to manoeuvre without being jostled.

Stemmed glasses are best for tasting and the ISO – International Standards Organisation – tasting glass is a good example. The sherry copita, the Paris goblet or the tulip glass are also considered suitable shapes. These are broad at the base and narrow at the top, to concentrate the smell as the drink is being swirled to release its bouquet.

Tasting glasses should be washed in plain hot water – detergents leave an odour – and dried and polished to a brilliance with fresh, clean cloths. Dirty cloths leave rancid odours and nowadays there is a trend for guests in restaurants to smell the empty wine glass before the wine is actually served. They do so in order to detect if there are any off odours which would adversely affect the aroma and taste of the wine.

Fig. 2.1 ISO glass showing the correct filling level for a tasting sample

Pour about 50 ml (2 fl oz) of the wine into the glass, which allows sufficient room for it to be swirled so the bouquet can be enhanced and appreciated.

Colour

Holding the glass by the stem, tilt it towards the light or a white background and appraise the colour, which should be clear and gleaming, never cloudy, faded or dull.

White wine

These wines range in colour from very pale with green tinges to deep gold. Watch out for any browning at the rim (miniscus) of the wine, as this will reveal that the wine is past its best or has oxidised.

Rosé wine

Such wines can be pink, deep pink or onion-skinned in colour, but essentially they should be bright and brilliant in the glass and never subdued-looking or brown.

Red wine

These wines progress from purple in extreme youth, to be ruby, garnet-red and slightly brown or brick red in old age. Reds are usually very intense in colour yet sumptuous in appearance.

Smell

Smell also known as nose, bouquet or aroma, is very much interrelated with taste. Swirl the wine in the glass. Wine glasses should have lips narrower than the bowl so that as the bouquet evaporates from the wine it becomes more concentrated as it reaches the rim of the glass. Take a good deep smell and, using your imagination, associate the smell with other previously experienced smells (*see* table below).

Grape	Association*
Cabernet Sauvignon	blackcurrants
Chardonnay	ripe melon, fresh pineapple
Chenin Blanc	apples
Gewürztraminer	tropical fruits such as lychees
Merlot	plum, damson
Nebbiola	prunes
Pinot Noir	strawberries, cherries, plums (depending on where grown)
Riesling	apricots, peaches
Sauvignon Blanc	gooseberries
Syrah	raspberries
Zinfandel	blackberries, bramble, spice

*Other aroma associations can be as diverse as pine trees, resin, vanilla, coffee, tea, herbs, smoke, toast, leather, cloves, cinnamon, nutmeg, ginger, mint, truffles, oak, figs, lilac and jasmine.

Taste

The taste of a drink is detected in different parts of the mouth but most essentially on the tongue. Sweetness is detected at the tip and centre of the tongue, acidity on the upper edges, saltiness on the sides and tip and bitterness at the back. When tasting a drink, consider the following characteristics:

- Sweetness and dryness will be immediately obvious;
- Acidity will be recognised by its gum-drying sensation, but in correct quantities acidity provides crispness and liveliness to a drink;
- Astringency or tannin content, usually associated with some red wines, will give a dry coating or furring effect especially on the teeth and gums.

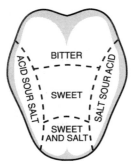

Fig. 2.2 How the tongue detects taste

Body, which is the feel of the wine in your mouth, and flavour, the essence of the wine as a drink, will be the final arbiters as to whether you like it or not. Aftertaste is the finish the wine leaves on your palate. Overall balance, the evaluation of all the above elements, can now be related to price.

When tasting more than five wines it is usual, for obvious reasons, to spit the wine out rather than swallow it. Take a small amount of the wine in the mouth together with a little air and roll it around so that it reaches the different parts of the tongue. Now lean forward so that the wine is nearest the teeth and suck air in through the teeth. This practice helps to highlight and intensify the flavour. At this stage and when you spit out the wine, the impressions made must be carefully noted otherwise you may get muddled and confused. Fortified wines are often appraised by sight and smell alone, as are brandies which, on occasion, can even be judged by rubbing a little of the spirit on the palm of the hand.

Observations

To help you analyse and make judgements on what you are tasting, here are some descriptive words that may be helpful:

Describing colour

Clear, bright, brilliant, gleaming, sumptuous, dull, grey, hazy, cloudy, pale, faded.

White wine
Water clear, pale yellow, yellow with green tinges, straw, gold, yellow-brown, maderised.

Rosé wine
Pale pink, orange-pink, onion-skin, blue-pink, copper.

Red wine
Purple, garnet, ruby, tawny, brick-red, mahogany.

Describing nose

Fruity, perfumed, full, deep, spicy, fine, rich, pleasant, nondescript, flat, corky.

Describing taste

Bone dry, dry, medium dry, medium sweet, sweet, luscious, unctuous, thin, light, medium, full-bodied, acid, bitter, spicy, hard, soft, silky, smooth, tart, piquant.

Summing up

Well balanced, fine, delicate, rich, robust, vigorous, fat, flabby, thick, velvety, harsh, weak, unbalanced, insipid, for laying down, just right, over the hill.

> It is important that you make up your own mind about the wine. Do not be too easily influenced by the observations of others.

Wine tastings

Wine tastings are very pleasant and effective ways of getting to know more about wine. Tastings are held for the purpose of appraising, assessing and appreciating the qualities of wine. They are organised on two levels – formal tastings and social tastings.

Formal tastings

These are organised by wine shippers or importers for the benefit of retailers and a selected public, including the Press. Attendance is free and by invitation only. The retailers will then, in turn, organise tastings for their customers and others, and wine societies may do likewise for their members. There may be a nominal charge for the entrance ticket, especially if food is also provided.

Social tastings

These are generally organised by private wine clubs. Very often there is a guest lecturer present to talk the participants through the tasting. More and more frequently social tastings take place among likeminded friends in their homes. Guests are each expected to bring an 'interesting bottle' while the hosts provide 'bites' or more ambitious fare and either the first or final wine of the evening.

How many wines?

The number of wines to be sampled is dictated by the basic requirements of the organisers and whether commercial orientation is involved. At a formal tasting, where selling is the bottom line, there may be between 20 and 100 (or more) wines for sampling. Social tastings can have as few as 5 wines and usually a maximum of 20 wines.

Styles of tasting

Tastings can take one of the following formats:

- General – where wines from different countries are 'shown' together;

- Ethnic – where wines from one particular country are to be assessed;
- Regional – where wines from a particular region are to be evaluated;
- Horizontal – where a number of different wines from the same vintage (year) are compared;
- Vertical – where comparisons of different vintages of the same wine are made;
- Competitive – also known as blind-tasting, where the identity of each wine is not known to the tasters and will not be revealed until the tasters' judgements and notes are handed in.

— Organising a wine tasting at home —

When setting up a wine tasting in your own home the following requirements are basic.

Format

Decide which format you want to follow (from those listed above).

Location

The room should be large enough to cope with the number of people invited. If artificial light is to be used, light bulbs are better than fluorescent tubes which tend to distort colours. If possible have a white background to facilitate colour examination. The temperature of the room should be comfortable – neither too cold nor too warm. There must be no distracting smells like perfume, aftershave, tobacco smoke or cooking odours from the kitchen, which would interfere with the bouquet of wine.

Time

The best time for tasting is before a meal when the palate is fresh and receptive. Most professional or formal tastings take place in the morning, from 11 a.m. onwards. But before dinner is also a good time as it accommodates those who work during the day.

Glasses

These should be brilliantly clean with no off-odours. The number required will depend on whether the tasting is a 'stand-up' or 'sit-down' style. Stand-up tastings will require a minimum of two glasses per person, one for white wine and one for red wine. At sit-down tastings allow one glass per wine per person. So, if there are six wines to be tasted there should be six glasses set before each individual.

Temperature

Wines must be offered at their correct serving temperatures. These ambient temperatures are given on page 29. Wines throwing sediment must be decanted (*see* page 27) beforehand and the bottles kept for inspection.

Tastings per bottle

Gauge for 8 to 12 as this allows guests to come back for a second opinion. If the wines are going to be blind-tasted conceal each label and give each bottle a number instead.

TASTING SHEET

A tasting sheet is very useful and can be prepared easily under the following headings:

Date and time of tasting....................Location.......................

Name of wine and vintage	Colour and clarity	Nose	Taste	Conclusions	Supplier and price

---

Order of tasting

The traditional order in which wines are tasted is:

- White wines before red wines, except in the case of sweet whites which are tasted last
- Dry wines before sweet wines
- Light before heavy
- Good before better

Spitoons

If you are tasting more than five wines it makes sense to spit out the samples after assessing them. For sit-down tastings individual receptacles are necessary – a funnel in an empty wine bottle will do nicely. For stand-up tastings shared receptacles are the practical answer. These can be plastic bowls or buckets or plastic-lined boxes or other containers half-filled with sawdust.

Adjuncts

These might include biscuits, bread, water, but no cheese as it tends to flatter wine. As they say in France 'sell [wine] on cheese, buy on apples'. And remember – **Think while you Drink**.

———— Sensible drinking ————

Drinking can have its problems. The great majority of the population who drink alcohol do so for many reasons: to quench a thirst, as a relaxant or simply because they like the stuff. But there's the rub: some people like it too well. It is reminiscent of the man who thought he had an alcohol problem until he found another bottle!

A small amount of alcohol does no harm and can even be beneficial. However, the more you drink and the more frequently you drink, the greater the health risks. Alcohol depresses the brain and nerve function, thereby affecting one's judgement, self-control and skills.

Most of the alcohol you drink passes into the bloodstream from where it is rapidly absorbed. (This absorption may be slowed down somewhat if drink is accompanied by food.) Almost all the alcohol must then be burnt up by the liver, with the remainder being disposed of in urine or perspiration. Someone once said that the liver is like a car with just one gear. It can burn up only one unit of alcohol in an hour so, if it has to deal with too much alcohol over the years, it will inevitably suffer damage.

So what are the sensible limits we can go to if we wish to avoid damaging our health? Of course, if you stop drinking alcohol you cut out any risk. However, medical expert opinion from the Royal College of Physicians sets the limit at 21 units a week (spread throughout the week) for men and 14 units a week (spread throughout the week) for women.

---

1 unit = 295 ml ($\frac{1}{2}$ pint) of ordinary beer or lager
or a glass of sherry
or a measure of vermouth or other apéritif
or one measure of spirits

From these guidelines we can see that if a man drinks 36 units or more of alcohol throughout the week (e.g. 10.5 litres (18 pints) of beer or $1\frac{1}{9}$ bottles of whisky) then he is likely to be damaging his health. Similarly, if a woman goes beyond 22 units (say $1\frac{1}{2}$ bottles of sherry) throughout the week, then a risk to her health is likely. Be very careful drinking at home or in somebody else's home. A generous hand can be too generous for your own good, so look carefully at the drink level in your glass.

Hangovers

George Bernard Shaw once said 'eat at leisure, drink by measure'. This is good advice. However, if you do go too far then remember every pleasure has a price; over-indulgence in alcohol leads to hangovers. A hangover is a headache resulting from (a) dehydration of the body caused by the alcohol, (b) the presence of congeners (additives, etc.) in the drink, and (c) lack of real sleep. This is why we suffer after a big drinking binge.

A hangover is an unpleasant experience and people are constantly searching for effective cures. However, as in so many things, prevention is always better than cure:

- It is always advisable to drink less and to eat well before an evening of drinking. Food lines the stomach and acts as a buffer against the war that alcohol wages;
- Avoid mixing drinks, if possible;
- Be wary of concoctions such as laced drinks, dubious punches, wine cups and foul, cheap wine;
- Drinks lots of water before you go and after you come from a heavy drinking party.

However, if you have failed to heed this advice and you feel absolutely rotten in the morning, try one of the following remedies:

- Prairie Oyster: into a glass put one egg yolk, one measure of brandy, one teaspoon wine vinegar, one teaspoon Worcester sauce and a little cayenne pepper. Drink in a gulp without breaking the yolk;
- If you do not have all the above ingredients at home, take a brisk walk to the chemist, inhaling deeply on your way, and ask for a dose of kaolin and morphine. This is a rather drastic solution, but it works;
- There are many proprietary brand bitters which will also do the trick or at least shock the system in the attempt. Underberg and Fernet Branca are particular favourites;
- The 'hair of the dog' – well why not, if you believe it will do you good!

Calories in alcohol

There are about 100 calories (420 kJ) in a single unit of alcohol. The amount of calories adds up quickly and can increase weight. However, replacing food with alcohol as a source of calories denies the body of essential nutrients and vitamins.

A guide to the number of calories found in a variety of drinks is given below. However, the number of calories in different brands of drinks can vary significantly, so the chart on the following page is only a rough guide.

		Calories	kJ
Fortified wines			
Sherry 50 ml measure	dry	55	230
	medium	60	250
	sweet	65	270
Wines			
113 ml (4 fl oz) glass	dry, white or red	75	315
	rosé	85	350
	sweet	100	420
Spirits			
25 ml measure	gin, whisky, vodka, rum, brandy	50	210
Beers, lagers and cider			
284 ml (10 fl oz) glass	lager, low alcohol	60	250
	light or mild ale	70	290
	brown ale	80	335
	lager	85	350
	bitter	90	375
	cider, dry	95	395
	cider, sweet	110	460
Non-alcoholic drinks			
tonic water 250 ml (9 fl oz)		35	145
low calories tonic water 250 ml (9 fl oz)		0	0
orange juice 180 ml (6 fl oz)		80	335
can of coke 330 ml (11.5 fl oz)		130	545
diet coke 330 ml (11.5 fl oz)		0	0

3

BUYING WINE

One of the pleasures of wine appreciation is gaining experience and confidence in buying wine. There are, however, some pitfalls to watch out for. This chapter offers some advice for buying in a restaurant and for the home. There are also some notes on the storage of wine.

In the restaurant

Wine lists, be they grandiose, printed and illustrated or a typed sheet in a folder, can in fact be very intimidating to the newcomer to wine. It is best to remember that they are merely a list of drinks held for sale in an establishment. Lists come in two styles: the restaurant list, which shows the complete range of beverages on offer, and the banquet list, which shows a more limited selection of the more commercial and popular items.

The pleasure of eating out is being enjoyed increasingly by more and more people, and the young especially are great experimenters in their choice of food and its subsequent marriage to wine. However, some people tend to shy away from wines with names that are difficult to pronounce, but a perceptive wine waiter will quickly gauge the situation, offering advice without causing embarrassment. It is often better to order wine by the bin number – each wine listed is given a certain number corresponding to the number under which the wine is stored in the cellar. So you simply order a bottle of number 10, or whatever.

Features of the wine list

Wines featured on the wine list should complement the menu both in style and price and should encourage the more adventurous to experiment with wines that may not be readily available in other commercial outlets. Rarely, however, except perhaps in the more deluxe restaurants, will customers purchase wine to accompany a meal when the price of the wine exceeds the price of the meal itself. Fair markups which become proportionately smaller as the wine gets more expensive will encourage people to experiment and buy good wine.

A wine list should also take into account those who dine alone or the couple with different preferences – one who likes white wine and the other red. Good wine, other than house wine, should be available by the glass and there should be some choice in half bottles. People on diets, organic wine lovers, those with illnesses such as diabetes, the ever increasing number who strive to lead healthy lifestyles and, of course, car drivers should all be catered for, and so low alcohol or de-alcoholised wines are a must nowadays on every drinks list.

The selection of wines does not have to be big to be good, but it should be well balanced, not only in terms of the country of origin but also of the grape used. Above all, it should be informative, giving the bin number, the name of the wine (sometimes with descriptive comments, if appropriate), the vintage year if applicable, the producer's, bottler's or shipper's name, whether the wine is bottled at source (i.e. estate or château bottled) and the price per magnum, bottle or half bottle.

The sequence in which the drinks are listed is traditional. First come the apéritifs, then the wines and other drinks and finally the digestifs. Wine lists can also be presented according to price bands.

Ordering wines

When ordering wines it is useful to seek the advice of the server. Well-trained servers will know the product on offer and will be pleased to discuss your selection with you. If you are going to order expensive wines, especially reds, then do try to do this in advance. It gives an opportunity for the establishment to ensure that it is properly temperated and for red wine to be decanted in advance if appropriate. Above all, don't be intimidated in restaurants. Drink what you like within your budget.

For the home

Wine is available in a variety of outlets. These include:

- off licences
- supermarkets
- local stores
- specialist wine merchants
- clubs and societies

The range of wines available and the prices can vary between these types of outlets. The advice that is offered can also vary. One of the most important aspects to consider is the confidence that you might have in a particular retailer. As your own experience and knowledge increases, this will become less important as you will be more confident of your own judgement.

Clubs and societies

It is certainly worth considering joining one of the clubs or societies. These include the Sunday Times Wine Club, The Wine Society and the Sunday Telegraph Wine Club. These clubs, as well as supplying a range of wines, provide regular useful information and a range of special offers. They can also offer useful advice on buying if you are considering laying any wines down.

Another advantage is that there is always the possibility of wine tours through these clubs and societies. A small number of travel companies offer tours to the wine regions. Visiting the regions brings the subject even more to life and can make a very enjoyable holiday – the rural areas are generally quite beautiful and restful.

Wine merchants

If you are going to buy from local wine merchants then it is worth spending time getting to know them. This will increase your confidence in them and will help them to understand that you are serious in your interest. This will also lead to the possibility of tastings and early advice on any specials that may be available.

Wine Taste Guide

One of the most useful general indicators of recent times is the Wine Taste Guide. This was devised by the Wine Development Board and accepted as standard within the industry. This is a quick and easy method of telling at a glance whether a white wine is bone dry or lusciously sweet. Very dry wines like the Chablis, are graded as 1: Moscatel is at the other extreme and is graded 9. The Wine Taste Guide also clarifies the degrees of sweetness in between. The Red Wine Taste Guide works in the same way but is based not on sweetness or dryness, but on fullness, so the biggest, richest reds rate at E: at the other end of the scale, light summery reds are classified as A. These indicators are found increasingly on displays and on the bottles.

Selection of wine

It is worth buying guides such as the *Pocket Wine Guide* by Hugh Johnson. This guide is particularly useful for descriptions of various wines and for vintage selection.

For laying down wines, that is buying wine and then storing it for drinking at a later time, some caution is suggested. There is always a risk. First, it is important that the wine you buy has some authority suggesting that the wine should and can be kept. Second, you must have appropriate storage available. Some merchants and clubs may provide this but at a cost.

Whether buying wine for drinking soon or for laying down, price is an important factor. Generally there is a direct relationship between the price and the quality of wine. The higher the price usually the higher the quality. However where there is limited availability of certain wines and demand is high, this will have had the effect of disproportionately increasing the price. In addition duty on wine tends to be per bottle, therefore higher priced wines will usually be better value. You will find that most retailers will offer a per case rate which is lower than the same number of bottles bought separately. This is often at the price of 11 bottles for a 12-bottle case. Some retailers will offer a discount on a case made up of different wines. Some also offer special selection deals where a case contains a range of pre-selected wines.

DRY TO SWEET WINE GUIDE

Number 1 signifies very dry white wines. Number 9 indicates maximum sweetness.
The numbers in between span the remaining dryness-to-sweetness spectrum.

| 1 Muscadet Champagne Chablis Dry White Bordeaux Manzanilla Sherry Tavel Rosé | 2 Soave White Burgundy Fino Sherry Sercial Madeira Rioja Penedès | 3 Brut Sparkling Wine Gewürztraminer d'Alsace Dry Amontillado Sherry Medium Dry Montilla Dry White Vermouth Anjou Rosé Medium Dry English | 4 Vinho Verde Mosel Kabinett Rhein Kabinett Laski and Hungarian Olasz Reisling, Medium Dry Portuguese Rosé |

| 5 Vouvray Demi-Sec Liebfraumilch Medium British Sherry Verdelho Madeira | 6 Demi-Sec Champagne Spanish Medium Sherry All Golden Sherry types | 7 Asti Spumante Rhein Auslesen Premières Côtes de Bordeaux Tokay Aszu Pale Cream Sherry Montilla Cream Bual Madeira Rosso, Rosé and Bianco Vermouths | 8 Austrian Beerenauslesen Spanish Sweet Wine Sauternes Barsac Cream and Rich Cream Sherry types | 9 Malmsey Madeira Muscat de Beaumes de Venise Marsala |

THE RED WINE GUIDE

The five categories marked A to E identify styles of red wines
in terms of light styles to big, full-bodied heavy wines.

A Bardolino Beaujolais Valdepeñas

B Côtes de Roussillon Merlot Navarra Pinot Noir from all countries Red Burgundy Valencia Valpolicella

C Bordeaux Rouge/Claret Côtes du Rhône Rioja

D Cabernet Sauvignon from Australia Bulgaria, California, Chile, New Zealand, Romania and South Africa Châteauneuf du Pape Chianti Dão Hungarian Red

E Barolo Crozes Hermitage Cyprus Red Greek Red Shiraz from Australia and South Africa

Fig. 3.1 Red and white wine guides (courtesy of Grierson's Wine Merchants)

Storage of wine

Ideally, wine should be stored in a subterranean cellar which has a northerly aspect and is free from vibrations, excessive dampness, draughts and unwanted odours. The cellar should be absolutely clean, well ventilated, with only subdued lighting and a constant cool temperature of 12.5°C (55°F) to help the wine develop gradually. Higher temperatures bring wines to maturity more quickly, but this is not preferable.

Table wines should be stored on their sides in bins so that the wine remains in contact with the cork. This keeps the cork expanded, moist and elastic, and prevents air from entering the wine – a disaster which quickly turns wine to vinegar. White, sparkling and rosé wines are kept in the coolest part of the cellar and in bins nearest the ground (because warm air rises). Red wines are best stored in the upper bins. Commercial establishments usually have special refrigerators or cooling cabinets for keeping their sparkling, white and rosé wine at serving temperature. These may be stationed in the dispense bar – a bar located between the cellar and the restaurant – to facilitate prompt service. Fortified wines are stored upright in their containers. The exceptions are port-style wines which are destined for laying down.

Only a few people are able to enjoy the benefits of a cellar, so a wine rack in a redundant fireplace or cupboard, or bins under the stairs have to suffice. It is important to locate your wine away from excessive heat – hot water pipes, a heating plant or hot water unit. Heat does far more damage to wine than the cold. Attractive humidity- and temperature-controlled cabinets are available, but they are expensive. Wine racks designed for the dining room may be decorative, but the constant changes in temperature in such rooms damage the wines. Evenness of temperature is essential. Attractive bins which hold up to 24 bottles are available, but empty wooden wine cases will serve equally as well.

4

WINE AND FOOD HARMONY

Nowadays the old maxim of red wine with meat and game, white with fish and poultry has given way to a much more relaxed attitude. People have broken away from the very rigid approach to the marriage of food and wine propounded by the wine pundits of yore to those who would listen. They are now much more inclined to drink what they like, when they like, and are much more open and honest about their wine preferences. If they do not care for red or dry white wines, they are not in the least bit intimidated by the raised eyebrows of the haughty wine waiter as they order the luscious Château Rieussec with their steak – and good for them, too!

Hosting a table either at home or in a restaurant presents a different situation, and here you can hope that your guests have more conventional tastes. However, it is a well-known fact that our choice of wine and other drinks is influenced by a variety of different factors: the occasion, the time of day and year, the weather, one's mood, the location, the theme of the event, the atmosphere, one's previous experience of the party, the food, the price, marketing and the media, the selling skills of the restaurant personnel and, of course, one's personal ego and preference.

General Guidelines

When selecting a wine to accompany a meal it is important to understand the compatibility of flavours and textures. This can be gleaned only through trial and error. However, there are certain guidelines that are worth observing:

- Dry wines should be served before sweeter wines;
- White wines should come before red wines;
- Lighter wines should be served before heavier wines;
- Good wines should appear before great wines;
- The main course wine should always be finished before the sweet course to prevent a clash of two different tastes, which will destroy the pleasant memory of the wine with the main course. This is one of the reasons why the French eat cheese before the sweet; the custom ensures that the main course wine is finished before the sweet course is served;
- Wine should not really be drunk with certain foods like chocolate, eggs, salads with vinegar dressings, mint sauce and very hot and spice foods such as curries. If an accompaniment is desired with these foods, then something inexpensive should be chosen since the food will flatten and dull the taste of the wine, if it does not completely overpower it.

However, when contemplating possible food and wine partnerships, remember that no guidelines exist to which there are not exceptions. For example, although fish is usually served with white wine, some dishes, such as heavily sauced salmon, red mullet or a fish such as lamprey (which is traditionally cooked in red wine), can be successfully accompanied by a slightly chilled red Saint-Emilion, Pomerol or Mercury. The combinations that prove most successful are those that please the individual.

—— Suggested combinations ——

Clearly, the matching of food and wine is highly subjective. However, the overall intention should be to provide food and wine which harmonise well together, each enhancing the other's performance.

Apéritifs

The purpose of an apéritif is to sharpen the palate and to start the gastronomic juices flowing in anticipation of the meal to come. Beware of excessive amounts of strong drinks such as spirits and cocktails. However enjoyable they may be at the time, they will deaden the palate for the wine and food that follow.

The name apéritif comes from the Latin *aperitivus* – to open out (in this case it is the gastric juices which are 'opened out' to give an appetite for the meal to come).

- Champagne, sherry, dry white wine, Madeira and vermouths are particularly good apéritifs, but they must not be drunk to excess, otherwise the food takes second place and is not likely to be appreciated;
- Gin with a variety of partners seem to be the most popular apéritif nowadays: gin and tonic, gin and It (Italian vermouth), gin and French (French vermouth) and, of course, the Martini cocktail (gin and dry vermouth) please most people. For those who dislike gin, vodka is the natural substitute;
- Schnapps and pastis are also popular, as are the various bitters;
- Whisky and soda, Kir, Buck's Fizz and sundry cocktails all help whet the appetite and get people in the mood for enjoying the meal;
- A more simple approach is to serve the wine that will accompany the first course.

Hors-d'oeuvre

- Fino or Manzanilla sherry
- Sancerre or Gewürztraminer

Soups

These do not really require a liquid accompaniment but sherry or dry port or Madeira could be tried. Consommés, turtle soup and lobster or crab bisque can be uplifted by adding a glass of heated sherry or Madeira before serving.

Foie gras

- Beaujolais or a light, young, red wine
- Some sweet wines

Cheese omelettes and quiches

Ideally, no wine should be served, but an Alsatian Riesling or Sylvaner is probably the most suitable if wine is required.

Farinaceous dishes (pasta and rice)

Nothing is better than Italian red wines such as Valpolicella, Chianti, Barolo, Santa Maddalena, or Lago di Caldaro.

Fish

- Oysters and shellfish: dry white wines, Champagne, Chablis, Muscadet, Soave and Frascati.
- Smoked fish: white Rioja, Hock, white Graves, Verdicchio
- Fish dishes with sauces: fuller white wines such as Vouvray, Montrachet or Yugoslav Riesling.
- Shallow fried, poached or grilled fish: Vinho Verde, Moselle, Californian Chardonnay, Australian Sémillon or Chardonnay.

White meats

The type of wine to serve is dependent on whether the white meat (chicken, turkey, rabbit, veal or pork) is served hot or cold:

- Served hot with a sauce or savoury stuffing: either a rosé such as Anjou, or light reds like Beaujolais, New Zealand Pinot Noir, Californian Zinfandel, Saint Julien, Bourg and Burgundy (e.g. Passe-tout-grains) and Corbières.
- Served cold: fuller white wines such as Hocks, Gran Viña Sol, Sancerre and the rosés of Provence and Tavel.

Other meats

- Duck and goose: big red wines that will cut through the fat, Châteauneuf-du-Pape, Hermitage, Barolo and the Australian Cabernet Shiraz
- Roast and grilled lamb: Médoc, Saint-Emilion, Pomerol and any of the Cabernet Sauvignons

- Roast beef and grilled steaks: big red Burgundies, Rioja, Barolo, Dão and wines made from the Pinot Noir grape
- Meat stews: lighter reds, Zinfandel, Côtes du Rhône, Clos du Bois, Bull's Blood, Vino Nobile di Montepulciano
- Hare, venison and game: reds with distinctive flavour, Côte Rôtie, Bourgeuil, Rioja, Chianti, Australian Shiraz, Californian Cabernet Sauvignon, Chilian Cabernet Sauvignon and fine red Burgundies
- Oriental foods, Peking duck, mild curry, tandoori chicken, shish kebab: Gewürztraminer, Lutomer Riesling, Vinho Verde, Mateus Rosé or Anjou Rosé.

Cheese

The wine from the main course is often followed through to the cheese course but, if not, almost any wine will do as cheese and wine go together like bread and butter. Having said that, you should still consider the type of cheese being served:

- Light, cream cheeses go well with full bodied whites, rosés and light reds;
- Strong, pungent (even smelly) and blue-veined varieties cry out for big reds like Bordeaux and Burgundy, or tawny, vintage or vintage-style ports and even luscious sweet whites.

Sweets and puddings

Most sweets and puddings are only barely comfortable with wines, perhaps because two sweet tastes in the mouth are almost too much of a good thing. However, certain wines can be recommended:

- Champagne works well with sweets and puddings;
- The luscious Muscats (de Beaumes-de-Venise, de Setúbal, de Frontignan, Samos), Sainte-Croix-du-Mont, Sauternes, Banyuls, Monbazillac, Tokay and wines made from late-gathered individual grapes in Germany all make a brave effort to satisfy. Despite this, it is perhaps preferable to save the wine until after the sweet course when it can be appreciated to the full.

Dessert (fresh fruit and nuts)

Sweet fortified wines, sherry, port, Madeira, Málaga, Marsala,

Commandaria, Yalumba Galway Pipe and Seppelt's Para compliment fruit and nuts.

Coffee

- Cognac and other brandies such as Armagnac, Asbach, Marc, Metaxa, Grappa, Oude Meester, Fundador, Peristiani VO31
- Good aged malt whiskies
- Calvados, sundry liqueurs and ports

Sample menus with suggested wines

We have concentrated on three-course meals which is as much as most people want to eat these days – and as much as any host or hostess would want to prepare especially if they work during the day. We have chosen typical menus and wines – the wines are shown in brackets – from six countries, England, France, Germany, Italy, Spain and the United States.

English Menu

Potted Morecambe Bay Shrimps

(Breaky Bottom Seyval Blanc, Sussex)

—— O ——

Roast Aylesbury Duckling

(Hidden Spring, Dark Fields – red – Sussex)

—— O ——

Queen of Puddings

(Conghurst Blush, Kent)

French Menu

Filet de Sole Véronique

Poached filet of sole in a white wine sauce with green grapes

(Chassagne Montrachet, Burgundy)

—— O ——

Carré d'Agneau en Croûte de Fines Herbes

Best end of lamb with a brioche and herb crust

(Château Canon, Saint-Emilion, Bordeaux)

—— O ——

Beignes Soufflés, Sauce Abricot

Choux-paste fritters with apricot sauce

(Monbazillac, Bergerac, South-West France)

German Menu

Hering Salat

Herring salad

(Bernkasteler Badstube, Mosel)

—— O ——

Schweinebraten mit Sauerkraut

Roast pork with pickled cabbage

(Oppenheimer Kreuz Kabinett, Rheinhessen)

—— O ——

Rhabarber Gelee mit Süsser Schlagsahne

Rhubarb jelly with sweetened whipped cream

(Forster Jesuitengarten Auslese, Pfalz)

Italian Menu

Asparagi al Burro e Parmigiano

Asparagus with butter and Parmesan cheese

(Albana di Romagna, Emilia-Romagna)

—— O ——

Stracotto alla Fiorentina

Florentine beef stew

(Vino Nobile di Montepulciano, Tuscany)

—— O ——

Tiramisu

A trifle of mascarpone cheese, savoiardi biscuits, egg yolks
and Marsala

(Glass of Marsala, Sicily or Asti Spumante, Piedmont)

Spanish Menu

Gambas al Agillo

Prawns cooked in oil and flavoured with garlic

(Gran Viña Sol, Penedès)

—— O ——

Paella Valenciana

Combination of chicken, pork, ham, beef, rice and peppers

(Marqués de Murrieta–red–Rioja)

—— O ——

Naranjas con Vino

Oranges marinaded in wine and flavoured with cinnamon and brandy

(Gran Codorníu, Metodo Tradicional, Barcelona)

United States Menu

Oysters Rockefeller

(Château Ste. Michelle Sauvignon Blanc, Washington State)

—— O ——

Medallions of Venison with Blueberry Sauce

(Stags' Leap Cabernet Sauvignon, California)

—— O ——

Pumpkin Pie

(Wagner's Ice Wine, New York State)

5

WINE-PRODUCING
COUNTRIES AND REGIONS

Algeria

Most of the wine produced is either red or rosé and made in three centres: Alger, Oran and Constantine. The reds are products of the
Carignan, Cinsault and Alicante-Bouschet grapes. The rosés are
made from the Cinsault and Grenache, and the little white that is
made comes from Ugni Blanc and Clairette de Provence grapes.

Traditionally, the wines were consumed at home or used to bulk up
blended French wines for sale to the colonies and elsewhere. Since the
French pull-out in 1962 quality and trade has diminished, although
Côteaux de Mascara, a big, rustic red wine, is still much favoured.

Argentina

Owing to the hot climate and little rainfall, Argentina has had to
develop a unique system of irrigation for the vine and other crops to
survive. They produce all manner of wines in huge quantities and,
until the Falklands trouble, they were making inroads into the
British market, especially with the reds.

Mendoza is the biggest and best region. Its output is almost three-
quarters of the national total. Other good locations are San Juan, Río
Negro, La Rioja and Juyjuy, part of Salta and Catamarca. Cabernet
Sauvignon, Malbec, Merlot, Pinot Noir, Tempranillo and Syrah are
the red wine grapes and the Riesling, Sauvignon Blanc and Pinot
Blanc are used to make white wine.

Trapiche, the largest winery in Argentina, makes an exceptionally good Cabernet Sauvignon, as do San Telmo, José Orfila and Bianchi. Crillon makes a still white called Embajador and a sparkling white called Monitor. Proviar makes a good sparkling wine that is marketed as Champania 'M. Chandon'.

Australia

It was thought that Australia tipped, as it is, on the edge of Asia, could never successfully compete in the British wine markets against our near and more traditional supply sources. Today, however, almost every wine shop and wine outlet stocks Australian wine and the range gets bigger, annually. The reason, of course, is that Australia produces excellent, good-value wines in a wide range of styles, sometimes blending two or more grape varieties to great advantage.

The Chardonnay, Gewürztraminer, Rhine Riesling, Sauvignon Blanc and Sémillon are the main white grapes, with the brown Muscat (Frontignac) for dessert wine. Red wines are made from Cabernet Sauvignon, Pinot Noir, Hermitage, Shiraz and Malbec grapes.

Labels are informative, stating the grape or combination of grapes used. Sometimes they can be tricky, for example 'C S Malbec' on a label would indicate a blend, in descending proportions, of three red grapes – Cabernet Sauvignon, Shiraz and Malbec. Generally, however, the labels are easy to understand, as long as they do not give too much technical information such as the *baumé* number (sugar level of the grape when picked), age in cask and date of bottling. Words like 'Private Bin', 'Reserve Bin' and 'Bin Number' may indicate that the wine comes from a single vineyard and is of superior quality.

The wines

Australian wines are made in New South Wales not far from Sydney; in Victoria near Melbourne; in the Barossa Valley, Clare Valley, Coonawarra, along the banks of the Murray River and around Adelaide, South Australia; in Queensland near Brisbane; in Western Australia, in the Swan Valley near Perth; and in Tasmania near Hobart and a few more places. Overleaf are listed some of the best producers of wine.

Sparkling wines

In Australia wines made by the méthode traditionnelle (méthode Champenoise) are called Champagne but may not be exported under this name. For special quality try Seppelt's Great Western (VIC), Kaiser Stuhl Special Reserve (SA) and Lindeman's Grand Imperator (NWS). Others are:

Angas Brut (SA)
McWilliams Brut (NSW)
Mildara Yellowglen (VIC)

Yalumba Brut de Brut (SA)
Tulloch Brut (NSW)
Hermskerk Jansz (TAS)

White wine

Enterprise Rhine Riesling (SA)
Henschke Rhine Riesling Spätlese (SA)
Leo Buring Rhine Riesling (SA)
Petaluma Rhine Riesling (SA)
Rosemount Estate Rhine Riesling (NSW)
Lindeman's Hunter River Riesling (NSW)
Château Tahbilk Riesling (VIC)
Quelltaler Grande Reserve Riesling (SA)
Leeuwin Estate Chardonnay (WA)
Rosemount Estate Chardonnay (SA)
Petaluma Chardonnay (NSW)
Drayton's Chardonnay (NSW)
Lake's Folly Chardonnay (NSW)

Rothbury Estate Chardonnay (NSW)
Saxonvale Chardonnay (NSW)
Tyrrell's Chardonnay (NSW)
Lindeman's Hunter River White Burgundy (NSW)
Wynn's Huntersfield White Burgundy (SA)
Lindeman's Hunter River Porphyry Sauternes (NSW)
McWilliams Mount Pleasant Sauternes (NSW)
Rosemount Estate Sauvignon Blanc (NSW)
Henschke Sémillon (SA)
Hill-Smith Estate Sémillon (SA)
Kaiser Stuhl Sémillon (SA)

Reds

Lindeman's Hunter River Burgundy (NSW)
Lindeman's Cawarra Claret (NSW)
Penfolds St Henri Claret (SA)
Yalumba Signature Blend Claret (SA)
Reynella Coonawarra Cabernet Shiraz (SA)

Penfolds Cabernet Shiraz (SA)
Wolf Blass Black Label Cabernet Shiraz (SA)
Brokenwood Hermitage Cabernet Sauvignon (NSW)
Penfolds Grange Hermitage (SA)
Tulloch Glen Elgin Estate Hermitage (NSW)

Saltram Mamre Brook Cabernet
  Shiraz (SA)
Seppelt Cabernet Shiraz (SA)
Petaluma Cabernet Shiraz (SA)

Capel Vale Shiraz (WA)
Pipers Brook Pinot Noir (TAS)
Moorilla Estate Pinot Noir
  (TAS)

The following produce high-quality Cabernet Sauvignon wines:

Château Reynella (SA)
Château Tahbilk (VIC)
Laira (SA)
Hardy's Reserve Bin (SA)
Penfold (SA)
Stanley Leasingham (SA)
Taltarni (VIC)

Rothbury Estate (NSW)
Wynns Coonawarra Estate (SA)
Brown Bros Milawa (VIC)
Lake's Folly (NSW)
Evans & Tate (WA)
Robinsons Family (Qld)
Jacob's Creek (SA)

Australian-style sherry

Mildara George (VIC)
Quelltaler Granfiesta Dry Pale (SA)

Yalumba Chiquita (SA)

Australian-style port

Hardy's Vintage (SA)
Kaiser Stuhl Jubilee Port (SA)
Lindeman's Macquarie (NSW)
Reynella Vintage (SA)

Seppelt Para (SA)
Yalumba Galway Pipe (SA)
Elsinore Vintage (Qld)
Château Clare (SA)

———— Austria ————

About three-quarters of Austrian wine is white, made mostly from the native grape Grüner Veltliner, with contributions also from the Rhine Riesling, Welschriesling, Weissburgunder (Pinot Blanc), Gewürztraminer, Müller-Thurgau and Muskat-Ottonel. Red wines when made, come from the Blauer Spätburgunder (Pinot Noir), Blaufränkisch, Portugieser and Saint Laurent grapes.

Since the infamous diethylene glycol wine scandal of 1985 a few perpetrators have caused substantial damage to the Austrian wine trade, which now shows a shortfall of 80 per cent of the export market. Let us hope that the reputable producers can withstand the inevitable financial stresses and strains, and that their good, stylish wine will soon reach the traditional markets as before.

The most popular white wine in Austria is Gumpoldskirchner made in a village near Baden, south of Vienna from special grapes not mentioned above. They are Rotipfler and Spätrot, blended in equal proportions. Further south of Vienna the really good red, Vöslauer, is made in the village of Bad Vöslau. Vineyards to the west of Vienna especially in the Wachau district produce fine white such as Dürnsteiner Katzensprung, Dürnsteiner Flohaxen, Lóiben Kaiserwein, Riede Lóibenberg, Kremser Kögl and Kremser Wachtberg.

Burgenland in the eastern part of Austria gets lots of sunshine and has ideal conditions for producing overripe grapes, which in extreme ripeness are known as *ausbruch*. A delicious example of this is the wine from Neusiedler See called Rust. Other good wines are the white styles Neuberger, Mörbischer, St Georgener Welschriesling and the light and fruity red Blaufränkischer.

In Steiermark in the southern corner of Austria they made a lovely blush-style wine called Schilcher, which results from very brief maceration of the grape skins. In West Steiermark the speciality is the onion-skin-coloured rosé called Zwiebelschilcher.

General wine styles

Bergwein	mountain vineyard wine
Heurigerwein	new wine, from the Vienna Woods district; released for sale on 11 November each year and sold by the jugful in bars (*Heurigen*)
Perlwein	semi-sparkling or spritzig wine
Reidwein	single vineyard wine
Schaumwein	fully sparkling wine such as Schlumberger Blanc de Blancs, made by the méthode traditionnelle
Schluckwein	(gulping wine), a thirst quencher
Schoppenwein	(swilling wine), a thirst quencher

Viticulturists in many parts of the world are indebted to Dr Lenz Moser, of Austria, who devised the high and wide method of vine cultivation, which is especially associated with white wine production. He introduced the practice of training the vines high and well spaced out so that tractors could be used to farm them.

Bulgaria

Moslem austerity frowned on the cultivation of the vine in Bulgaria for many centuries. In 1944, the government recognised that wine could be a valuable export and encouraged the planting of vineyards, introducing best-quality grapes and modern methods of viticulture and vinification.

Although Bulgaria is only fourteenth in the table of producers it is actually the fourth largest exporter. The wines are very good and reasonably priced. They are matured in oak cask – whites for up to 18 months and the reds for 3 years. Whites to look out for are Dimiat, Riesling, Chardonnay, Sauvignon Blanc and Misket, and the reds Gamza, Mavrud, Melnic and Cabernet Sauvignon all are generous, soft and rounded in flavour.

Canada

Ontario is by far the biggest and most important wine region producing some 85 per cent of Canada's total. Much of the wine comes from the *Vitis labrusca* family (Concorde, Catawba, Delaware, Niagara and President). In more recent times the *Vitis vinifera* varietals such as Aligoté, Chardonnay, Gewürztraminer and the Johannisberg Riesling for whites and the Pinot Noir and Gamay for reds have been cultivated.

The major producers are:

Calona Wines Ltd	Andres Wines
Brights Wines	Château des Charmes
Château-Gai Wines	Colio Wines
Inniskillin Wines	London Winery
(one of the best names)	Montravin Cellars
Reif Winery Inc	Willowbank Estate

Besides the red and white table wines, dessert-style wines including Eiswein, and a substantial amount of sparkling wines are made.

Chile

Although Chile was one of the few places to dodge the *Phylloxera vastatrix* scourge, they restocked their vineyards in the mid nineteenth century with the finest of the noble varietal European vines. The resulting improvement in quality has elevated the red wines, especially the Cabernet Sauvignons, to world class level. Look out for this style from Concha y Toro, Cousino-Macul, Miguel Torres and Santa Rita. They are full, rich and velvet smooth, certain to please both palate and pocket. The best Chilean wines come from the Maipo and Aconcagua valleys.

Reds are also produced either as blenders, or in their own right, from Cabernet Franc, Malbec, Merlot and Pinot Noir grapes. Torres also produces a good rosé from the Cabernet Sauvignon grape and a refreshing sparkling white made by the méthode traditionnelle. The still whites have not, as yet, reached the same high standards as the reds but again Torres Sauvignon Blanc has good balance and elegance. The Chardonnay and Sémillon grapes are also used to produce sound if not spectacular whites.

Label language

Envasado en Origen	estate bottled
Viñas Courant	one year old
Viñas Special	two years old
Viñas Reserva	four years old
Viñas Reservado	six years old

China

China makes some rice 'wine' and white grape wines called Dynasty, Heavenly Palace and Great Wall. A sweet wine called Meikuishanputaochu is also made, as is a reasonable red wine called Cabernet d'Est. Climatic conditions are against quality.

Cyprus

The sunshine island of Cyprus produces a glistening selection of wines running from dry, medium and the more popular sweet sherries, to the renowned dessert wine, Commandaria. Although the sherries, are the more popular, Commandaria, reckoned to be the oldest known wine in the world, has more distinction. Made by farmers in 11 villages on the southern slopes of the Troodos mountains, the grapes are left to dry on roadsides and on rooftops for 10 to 15 days. They are then pressed and the new wine is kept until spring when it is sold to the wine establishments at Paphos and Limassol. Here it is flavoured with cloves, resin, scented wood, and fortified with local brandy.

Commandaria has a reputation for promoting longevity and is drunk locally as a tonic – some excuse! All we know is that this honey-sweet, amber-red wine is delicious after a meal. Try Commandarie St John. The island also produces good table wines.

Light whites

Amathus, Arsinoe, Palomino

Medium whites

Aphrodite, Bellapais (white and rosé semi-sparkling) and a newcomer, Thisbe, which has a nice nose and a smooth flavour.

Sweet whites

Hirondelle, St Hilarion and St Panteleimon

Rosé wine

The best is Coeur de Lion; the newish Amorosa is also good, as is Kokkineli, a deep rosé wine.

Red wine

Of the reds Kykko, Olympus and Salamis are nicely mellow, Agravani is dry and flavoursome, while Afames, Kolossi and Othello are full-bodied and fragrant.

Sparkling wine

Of the sparkling wines two that are agreeable and easy to remember are Avra and Duc de Nicosie. Watch for the names of the following wineries on Cyprus labels: Keo, Etko, Sodap and Loel.

England

The English have a hang-up about their wines. For some reason, many wine merchants seem reluctant to promote or even feature English wines on their lists, while the bigger and more established merchants will offer only one example, perhaps two at the most. Likewise with restaurant wine lists, most are devoid of English wines, and those that do show some often discourage sales by unreasonable mark-ups. This is all a great pity because English wine is good, if not great, and accompanies lighter food dishes more than adequately. 'English' wines are made from grapes grown in England alone. Wines labelled 'British' are made from imported unfermented grape juice (must) and may not be called 'English' wines.

The vine was first introduced into Britain by the Romans, and the 1086 Domesday Book survey recorded the existence if 83 vineyards. This number slowly increased, most being in the hands of monasteries, religious orders or great houses. When Eleanor of Aquitaine married Henry II in 1152 part of her dowry was the lands of Bordeaux which England owned thereafter for some 300 years. The red wine of Bordeaux was markedly superior to the wines of England and this fact, together with the dissolution of the monasteries in the 1530s, resulted in many vineyards falling into disuse.

It was not until well after the end of the Second World War that the English wine industry resurfaced physically and commercially. Today in England and Wales there are more than 300 vineyards occupying over 405 hectares (1,000 acres), producing mainly white wines from Germanic vine strains. These strains are especially suited to cold, northerly vineyards, with the extreme limit of cultivation being a rough line across the country from The Wash. The cold climate is a great problem, as are the wet summers such as in 1984 when a third of the crop was lost. The English winegrowers, as needs be, are a hardy and stubborn lot. Their fortitude is occasionally rewarded with a great vintage like that of 1989 when 3.2 million litres were produced (4.26 million bottles).

Experience has shown that the following vines produce the best white wine: Müller-Thurgau, Schönburger, Ortega, Reichensteiner, Huxelrebe, Bacchus, Gütenborner, Seyve Villard, Morio Muscat, Riesling and Sylvaner, and a French hybrid, Seyval Blanc. There are also red and rosé wines made from Pinot Noir, Zweigeltrebe and Gamay grapes, but so far they have not developed beyond the ordinary.

Look out for the EVA quality seal which is awarded annually by the English Viticultural Association to wines that are submitted for official testing. The EVA was formed in 1965 and their seal on a bottle indicates quality.

Major English vineyards

Adgestone (Isle of Wight)
Ascot (Berkshire)
Barton Manor (Isle of Wight)
Beaulieu (Hampshire)
Biddenden (Kent)
Bothy (Oxfordshire)
Breaky Bottom (Sussex)
Bruisyard (Suffolk)
Carr Taylor (Sussex)
Cavendish Manor (Suffolk)
Chilford Hundred (Cambridgeshire)
Chilsdown (Sussex)
Ditchling (Sussex)
Elmham Park (Norfolk)

English Wine Centre (Sussex)
 – sells a range of English wines
Hambledon (Hampshire)
Lamberhurst (Kent)
Merrydown (Sussex)
Pilton Manor (Somerset)
Tenterden and Spots Farm (Kent)
Staple (Kent)
Thames Valley (Berkshire)
Three Choirs (Gloucestershire)
Wellow (Hampshire)
Wootton (Somerset)
Wraxall (Somerset)

France

The glorious wine gardens of France produce a diversity of wine styles, generally of noble quality. Besides the excellent natural aspects of soil and climate, quality is controlled at all stages of production. The making and labelling of French wine is now governed by EU wine laws and defined as follows:

Vins de Qualité produits dans des regions determinées (VQPRD)

These are quality wines produced from grapes grown in specific regions. They are subdivided into two categories:

Vins d'appellation d'origine contrôlée (AOC)

This labelling guarantees:

- area of production
- grape varieties used
- pruning and cultivation methods
- maximum yield per hectare
- minimum alcohol content
- methods of vinification and preservation

Vins délimités de qualité supérieure (VDQS)

These are wines of superior quality produced in delimited areas with the following conditions guaranteed:

- area of production
- grape varities used
- minimum alcohol content
- methods of viticulture and vinification

Although the wines have to be good to merit the VDQS label, they are less fine than the AOC wines.

Vins de table

The second labelling category, Vins de table, is also divided into two:

Vins de pays (VP)

Local or country wine. Medium in quality, these wines must be made from recommended grapes grown in a certain area or village. They must have a minimum alcohol content, and come from the locality stated on the label.

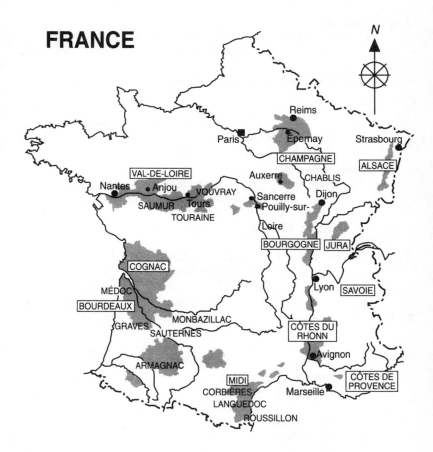

Fig. 5.1 Wine-producing regions of France

Vins de consommation courante (VCC)

Wines for everyday consumption and sold by the glass, carafe or *pichet* in cafés and bars all over France. Often completely authentically French, these wines may also be blended with other EU wines of similar style. Non-EU wines may not be blended with French wines.

Label language

Appellation d'origine contrôlée (AOC)	associated with the best French wines and guarantees origin of wine named on the label
Crémant	sparkling wine, but not Champagne
Cru	(growth) – used to describe a single vineyard; *Grand cru* and *premier grand cru* indicate higher and highest quality vineyards
Cuvée	blend or contents of a vat of wine
Château/domaine	estate
Cuve close	sparkling wine made in bulk inside a sealed vat
Millesime	vintage date
Mis en bouteille au château/domaine	bottled at the estate
Mis en bouteille dans nos caves/chais	bottled in our cellars, usually by a large wine company: not estate bottled
Mis en bouteille à la propriété par	bottled at the property or estate for somebody else, usually a wine dealer
Méthode Champenoise	Champagne method used in making some sparkling wines; now known as méthode traditionnelle
Moelleux	sweetish and smooth
Mousseux	sparkling
Négociant	wine handler who buys bulk wine from growers and sells it under his own label
Pétillant	lightly sparkling
Propriétaire, Récoltant	owner, grower
Récolte . . .	harvested . . . – followed by the vintage year
Sec	dry (*demi-sec*: medium dry and *doux*: sweet)
Sur lie	wine left to mature on its lees (sediment) before being bottled
Vendange tardive	late harvested grapes which produce sweeter wine

Vin de pays	a local wine usually of sound quality
Vin de table	*Vin ordinaire* – ordinary table wine
Vin délimité de qualité supérieure	(VDQS) wine of superior quality produced in the region as stated on the label
Vin doux naturel	(VDN) – sweet wine whose fermentation has been muted by the addition of alcohol
Vin Primeur	(*Vin de l'année, Vin nouveau*) wine made to be drunk within a year

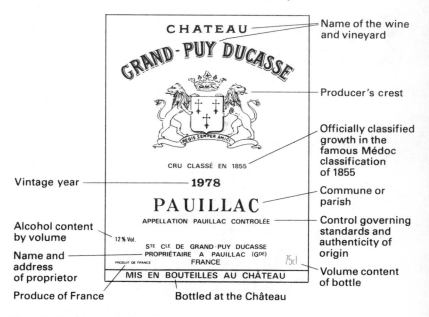

Fig. 5.2 French wine label

Alsace

Alsace wines are mainly white after the style of German Rhine wines and are marketed in tall green *flûte d'Alsace* bottles under grape rather than place names. Alsace Riesling is probably the most popular wine but other grapes used are Gewürztraminer, Pinot Gris (Tokay), Pinot Blanc (Klevner), Muscat and Sylvaner. The Pinot Noir is used to make a little red and a rosé known as Clairet d'Alsace or Schillerwein. There is also a white wine, Alsace Edelzwicker, made from a blend of noble grapes such as Riesling, Sylvaner, etc. The very pleasant sparkling Crémant d'Alsace is made mostly from a combination of Riesling and Pinot grapes. Alsace wines have variety in style and flavour and are reliably well made. The region is also famous for its Alcool Blanc, notably Eau-de-Vie de Poire William.

Bordeaux

Ever since 1152, when Henry II of England married Eleanor of Aquitaine and got Gascony and most of South-West France as a

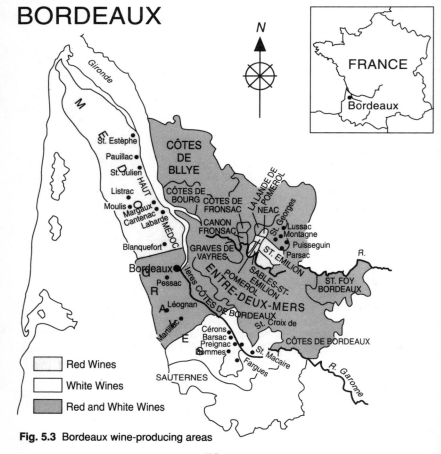

Fig. 5.3 Bordeaux wine-producing areas

dowry, the wines of Bordeaux have usually held pride of place in English cellars. Until 1453 the area was a part of the English crown and Claret, the red wines of Bordeaux, quickly became popular with Royal patronage.

Some 70 per cent of the total production are AOC quality of which two-thirds are red and one-third white. The red wines are made from the Cabernet Sauvignon, Cabernet Franc, Merlot, Malbec and Petit-Verdot grapes and the whites from the Sémillon, Sauvignon blanc and Muscadelle grapes. The main wine growing areas are: Médoc, Saint-Emilion, Pomerol, Entre-Deux-Mers, Graves, Cérons, Sauternes, and Bourg, Blaye and Fronsac.

Médoc

The most famous area in the world for the production of quality, long-lasting red wines. The area is so renowed for fine wines that in 1855, 61 of the better wines were classified into five division known as crus, or growths, and that classification, with just a few exceptions, holds good to this day.

Grands Crus Classés of the Médoc
The official classification of 1855

	Vineyard	Commune
First growths (Premiers crus)	Ch. Lafite-Rothschild	Pauillac
	Ch. Latour	Pauillac
	Ch. Margaux	Margaux
	Ch. Mouton-Rothschild	Pauillac[1]
	Ch. Haut-Brion	Pessac [2]
Second growths (Deuxièmes crus)	Ch. Rausan-Ségla	Margaux
	Ch. Rauzan-Gassies	Margaux
	Ch. Léoville-Lascases	St Julien
	Ch. Léoville-Poyférré	St Julien
	Ch. Léoville-Barton	St Julien
	Ch. Dufort-Vivens	Margaux
	Ch. Gruaud-Larose	St Julien

[1]Upgraded from the second to the first growth in 1973
[2]Graves District

Ch. Lascombes	Margaux
Ch. Brane-Cantenac	Cantenac
Ch. Pichon-Longueville-Baron	Pauillac
Ch. Pichon-Longueville-Lalande	Pauillac
Ch. Ducru-Beaucaillou	St Julien
Ch. Cos-d'Estournel	St Estèphe
Ch. Montrose	St Estèphe

Third growths	Ch. Kirwan	Cantenac
(Troisièmes crus)	Ch. d'Issan	Cantenac
	Ch. Lagrange	St Julien
	Ch. Langoa Barton	St Julien
	Ch. Giscours	Labarde
	Ch. Malescot-Saint-Exupéry	Margaux
	Ch. Boyd-Cantenac	Cantenac
	Ch. Palmer	Cantenac
	Ch. La Lagune	Ludon
	Ch. Desmirail	Margaux
	Ch. Cantenac-Brown	Cantenac
	Ch. Calon-Ségur	St Estèphe
	Ch. Ferrière	Margaux
	Ch. Marquis-d'Alesme-Becker	Margaux

Fourth growths	Ch. Saint-Pierre-Sevaistre	St Julien
(Quatrièmes crus)	Ch. Talbot	St Julien
	Ch. Branaire-Ducru	St Julien
	Ch. Duhart-Milon Rothschild	Pauillac
	Ch. Pouget	Cantenac
	Ch. La Tour-Carnet	St Laurent
	Ch. Lafon-Rochet	St Estèphe
	Ch. Beychevelle	St Julien
	Ch. Prieuré-Lichine	Cantenac
	Ch. Marquis-de-Terme	Margaux

Fifth growths	Ch. Pontet-Canet	Pauillac
(Cinquièmes crus)	Ch. Batailley	Pauillac
	Ch. Haut-Batailley	Pauillac
	Ch. Grand-Puy-Lacoste	Pauillac
	Ch. Grand-Puy-Ducasse	Pauillac
	Ch. Lynch-Bages	Pauillac

Ch. Lynch-Moussas	Pauillac
Ch. Dauzac	Labarde
Ch. Mouton Baronne Philippe	Pauillac
Ch. du Tertre	Arsac
Ch. Haut-Bages-Libéral	Pauillac
Ch. Pédesclaux	Pauillac
Ch. Belgrave	St Laurent
Ch. Camensac	St Laurent
Ch. Cos-Labory	St Estèphe
Ch. Clerc-Milon-Rothschild	Pauillac
Ch. Croizet-Bages	Pauillac
Ch. Cantemerle	Macau

Saint Emilion

Another famous red wine district was classified in 1955 and revised in 1969 and 1985. The wines are full and rounded with Château Ausone and Château Cheval Blanc being fine examples.

The 1955 classification
First great growths (Premiers grands crus)

Ch. Ausone
Ch. Cheval-Blanc } Grade A

Ch. Beauséjour-Duffau-
    Lagarrosse
Ch. Beau-Séjour-Bécot
Ch. Belair
Ch. Canon
Ch. Figeac
Clos Fourtet
Ch. La Gaffelière
Ch. La Magdelaine
Ch. Pavie
Ch. Trottevieille
} Grade B

Pomerol

A neighbouring district, to the west of Saint-Emilion, produces rich meaty but smooth reds; Château Pétrus is the best known. These wines were never officially classified but some of the better ones are listed below:

Cru exceptionnel	Château Pétrus
Other principal crus	Ch. Certan de May
	Ch. Certan-Giraud
	Ch. la Conseillante
	Ch. l'Eglise-Clinet
	Ch. l'Evangile
	Ch. la Fleur Pétrus
	Ch. la Grave-Trigant-de-Boisset
	Ch. Latour ų Pomerol
	Ch. Petit-Village
	Ch. le Pin
	Ch. Trotanoy
	Clos de l'Eglise (Moreau)
	Vieux Ch. Certan

Entre-Deux-Mers

A stretch of land between the two rivers Garonne and Dordogne produces decent reds plus dry and sweet white wines. AOC is at present limited to the dry white wines; the others may be sold as Bordeaux or Bordeaux Supérieure.

Graves

This district gets its name from the gravel content of the soil and was classified in 1959. Both red and white wines are made, although it is the reds that have the better reputation, especially the outstanding Château Haut-Brion which was nominated as a premier cru (first growth) wine in the famous 1855 classification of the Médoc.

Classified growths of the Graves		
Red wines	Ch. Boscaut	Cadaujac
(classified in	Ch. Haut-Bailly	Léognan
1953 and	Ch. Carbonnieux	Léognan
confirmed	Domaine de Chevalier	Léognan
in 1959)	Ch. Fieuzal	Léognan
	Ch. Olivier	Léognan

	Ch. Malartic-Lagravière	Léognan
	Ch. La Tour-Martillac	Martillac
	Ch. Smith-Haut-Lafitte	Martillac
	Ch. Haut-Brion	Pessac
	Ch. La Mission-Haut-Brion	Pessac
	Ch. Pape Clément	Pessac
	Ch. Latour-Haut-Brion	Talence
White wines (classified in 1959)	Ch. Bouscaut	Cadaujac
	Ch. Carbonnieux	Léognan
	Domaine de Chevalier	Léognan
	Ch. Olivier	Léognan
	Ch. Malartic-Lagravière	Léognan
	Ch. La Tour-Martillac	Martillac
	Ch. Laville-Haut-Brion	Talence
	Ch. Couhins	Villenave d'Ornon

Cérons

This area is on the borders of Graves, producing white fragrant wines which vary in style from dry to extremely sweet.

Sauternes

This district produces the most remarkable naturally sweet, golden wine you can taste. It is due to a phenomenon called *Botrytis cinerea*, also known as *pourriture noble* or noble rot. In autumn the local climatic conditions of morning moisture followed by the strong heat create the humidity that encourages spores to form and fester on the outside of the grape skins. The resulting fungus feeds on the moisture within each grape, gradually reducing the contents by two-thirds and, at the same time, concentrating the remaining juices into a rich sugar syrup. The dehydrated grapes are picked only when they have reached a specific state of rotting, so the vineyards are gone over time and time again. The resulting wine, luscious with creaminess and intense sweetness, has a vigour about it that stands it apart from other sweet wines. This quality is best exemplified by the famous Château d'Yquem.

Fig. 5.4 Grapes affected by *Botrytis cinerea* (noble rot)

Also within the limitations of the Sauternes boundaries are the regions of Barsac, Bommes, Fargues and Preignac, all producing very good sweet wines.

Sauternes and Barsac
The 1885 classification

First great growth (Premier grand cru)	Ch. d'Yquem	Sauternes

First growths (Premiers crus)	Ch. La Tour-Blanche	Bommes
	Ch. Lafaurie-Peyraguey	Bommes
	Clos Haut-Peyraguey	Bommes
	Ch. Rayne-Vigneau	Bommes
	Ch. Suduiraut	Preignac
	Ch. Coutet	Barsac
	Ch. Climens	Barsac
	Ch. Guiraud	Sauternes
	Ch. Rieussec	Fargues
	Ch,. Rabaud-Promis	Bommes
	Ch. Sigalas-Rabaud	Bommes

Second growths (Deuxièmes crus)		
	Ch. de Myrat	Barsac*
	Ch. Doisy-Daęne	Barsac
	Ch. Doisy-Dubroca	Barsac
	Ch. Doisy-Védrines	Barsac
	Ch. D'Arche	Sauternes
	Ch. Filhot	Sauternes
	Ch. Broustet	Barsac
	Ch. Nairac	Barsac
	Ch. Caillou	Barsac
	Ch. Suau	Barsac
	Ch. de Malle	Preignac
	Ch. Romer	Fargues
	Ch. Lamothe	Sauternes

* No longer in production

Bourg, Blaye and Fronsac

These are three areas producing white and red wines, but they are probably best known for their bright, full-bodied robust reds of Cru Bourgeois quality.

Burgundy

The vineyards of Burgundy stretch from Chablis in the far north to Lyon in the south, producing in good years white and red wines of excellence. However, in some years the grapes in the more northerly limitations do not ripen properly and wine producers take over from nature to add sugar to the must in order to bring the alcohol content up to that of a similar wine produced in a good year. This doctoring of the wine is legal and is known as chaptalisation after Dr Chaptal (1756–1832) who first introduced the practice. Chaptalised wines cannot be sold as vintage wines – they do not even bear that stamp of class and are often sold as second name wines or co-operative wines. This means that a vintage on a Burgundy label really means something.

Before 1789 most of the vineyards belonged to the Church but in the French Revolution they were seized and fragmented into saleable lots or *climats* which local farmers could afford to buy. Multi-ownership of original vineyards has been a tradition ever since; in fact, one famous vineyard, Clos de Vougeot, is owned by 85 growers, each entitled to sell his wine by the vineyard name. With the sugaring of the must and the dissecting of vineyards, the buying of Burgundy can at times be something of a gamble!

Owing to their popularity in countries such as America, Belgium and Great Britain, there is a perpetual shortage of the finest Burgundies (which are sold at very high prices). Many of the finest wines are domaine bottled by the grower and sold under the vineyard or *commune* (parish) label. Much is also sold to *négociants* who prepare a

Fig. 5.5 Burgundy wine-producing areas

blend of several wines thereby averaging the quality as well as the price. It is, therefore, advisable to acquaint oneself with the names of reliable négociants or shippers such as Patriarche, Bouchard Père et Fils, Joseph Drouhin, Georges Duboeuf, Louis Jadot, and Louis Latour when considering Burgundy.

Of all the wine produced, five-sixths is red and only one-sixth white. The great reds are made from the classic Pinot Noir grape and others from the Gamay or Passe-tout-grains (a mixture of one-third Pinot Noir and two-thirds Gamay). The excellent whites are produced from Chardonnay grapes and the less fine from the Aligoté. Burgundy is divided into six regions: Chablis, Côte de Nuits, Côte de Beaune, Côte Chalonnaise, Côte Mâconnaise and Beaujolais.

Chablis

The flinty dry white wines coming from this district have attained the greatest possible distinction, being generally regarded as the best accompaniment to shellfish and light delicate foods. Going from basic to brilliant, the wines are classified as Petit Chablis, Chablis, Chablis Premier Cru and Chablis Grand Cru. The latter has seven vineyards of the highest calibre:

Vaudésir	Grenouilles	Blanchots
Les Preuses	Les Clos	Les Bougros
Valmur		

Côte de Nuits

A red wine district of great renown producing full-bodied meaty wines which develop gradually into silky smooth wines of exceptional class. Some examples of the famous communes and outstanding vineyards are shown in the table below.

Commune	Vineyard
Gevrey-Chambertin	Chambertin
	Clos de Bèze
Morey Saint-Denis	Clos de Tart
	Clos Saint-Denis
Chambolle Musigny	Musigny
	Les Bonnes-Mares

Vougeot	Clos de Vougeot
Flagey-Echézeaux	Echézeaux
	Grand Echézeaux
Vosne Romanée	La Romanée-Conti
	Le Richebourg
	La Romanée Saint-Vivant
Nuits-Saint-George	Les Saint-Georges
	Clos de la Maréchale

Côte de Beaune

This district is famous for fine, but less assertive, supple reds which age in a reasonably short time. Quality white wines are also produced.

Côte de Beaune reds

Commune	Vineyard
Pernand-Vergelesses	Les Vergelesses
Aloxe Corton	Le Corton
	Corton Clos du Roi
Savigny-les-Beaune	Les Lavières
Beaune	Les Marconnets
	Le Clos de Mouches
Pommard	Les Epinots
	Les Rugiens
Volnay	Les Caillerets
	Les Champans
Santenay	Les Gravières
	Le Clos de Tavannes
Chassagne-Montrachet	Clos Saint-Jean

> Côte de Beaune can be a combination wine from the Beaune area.
> Côte de Beaune Villages comes from one or more villages which have a right to the appellation.

Côte de Beaune whites

Commune	Vineyard
Meursault	Les Perrières-Dessous
	Les Charmes-Dessous
Puligny-Montrachet	Le Montrachet
Chassagne-Montrachet	Le Chavalier Montrachet
	Le Batard Montrachet
	(overlaps both communes)
Aloxe Corton	Le Corton-Charlemagne

Côte de Beaune whites are celebrated for their superb style and quality, the finest being produced in the Montrachet and neighbouring Meursault vineyards. However, there are also other fine wines from Côte de Beaune, for example Corton-Charlemagne (Aloxe Corton).

Beaune is also known for its Hospices de Beaune, a fifteenth-century almshouse which looks after pensioners and the poor. The hospital was founded in 1443 by the then Chancellor Nicolas Rolin who endowed the premises with vineyards and encouraged others to be benefactors in like manner. The sale of wines from these vineyards supports the Hospices and, since 1859, on the third Sunday of each November a famous wine auction takes place in public; this is its chief source of income. Each lot of wine is auctioned *à la chandelle*: the bidding starts when the auctioneer lights a candle, which is snuffed when the lot is sold. Another candle is then lit to start the bidding for the next lot. Usually just two candles are used. The prices realised, although benevolently generous, set a standard for Burgundy prices for that particular year.

> The Côte de Nuits and Côte de Beaune are together popularly known as the Côte d'Or (Golden Hillsides), not only because of the beautiful vista of their gold-coloured vineyards in the autumn but also because of the wealth that the wines have generated.

Côte Chalonnaise

This district produces lighter red wines which mature quickly but lack the grandeur of the Côte d'Or wine. Mercurey, Rully and Givry are the best examples while Montagny, made exclusively from Chardonnay grapes, and Bouzeron are the best of the white wines made.

Côte Mâconnaise

This region is a prolific producer of light, red, fruity wines – pleasant wines for picnics, wine and cheese parties and the like. They are usually sold as Mâcon Rouge or Mâcon Supérieur and the latter must have an alcohol content of 11 per cent.

By far the best Mâconnais wine is the white Pouilly Fuissé made from Chardonnay grapes in the communes of Fuissé, Salutré, Vergisson and Chaintré. Adjoining communes, Pouilly-Vinzelles and Pouilly-Loché, also produce these typically fine fresh and vigorous wines while the appellation Mâcon-Villages (Blanc) has sound whites such as Mâcon Lugny, Mâcon Prissé and Mâcon Clessé. Saint Véran, made in vineyards which overlap Mâcon and Beaujolais, is similar in style.

Beaujolais

Although some good white wine is made in Beaujolais, it is the light, fruity aromatic reds that give the area fame and fortune. Most wines are sold under the parish name of origin (Beaujolais Cru):

Saint-Amour	Juliénas
Chénas	Chiroubles
Morgon	Moulin-à-Vent
Brouilly and Côte de Brouilly	Fleurie
	Régnié

Genuine Beaujolais is made in huge quantities from Gamay grapes and ranges in quality from basic Beaujolais, Beaujolais Supérieur to Beaujolais Villages (a blend of wine from two villages or more).

The vogue for Beaujolais Nouveau (Beaujolais Primeur) accounts for half the Beaujolais sales. This light but pleasant swilling wine is made by a method called *macération carbonique*. The whole bunches, together with their stalks, are piled in a closed vat or container and the grapes are left to press themselves. As the weight of the grapes releases the juice, natural fermentation begins to take place within each grape. Later the process is completed according to local tradition resulting in a wine which is soft, fragrant, fruity and ready for drinking once bottled. It is released for sale on the third Thursday in November and is best drunk between then and Christmas. Beaujolais de l'Année is somewhat different being offered for sale within a year of its vintage.

Beaujolais is at its most refreshing when drunk at cellar temperature – slightly chilled.

Champagne

Champagne is a protected name and is unquestionably the greatest of all sparkling wines. The vineyards are located in north-east France and cover some 21,000 hectares (51,870 acres). The three demarcated areas are Montagne de Reims, Vallée de la Marne and Côte des Blancs (the white hillsides near Épernay which are planted with the white Chardonnay grape, hence the name).

Besides Chardonnay, which gives an attractive crispness, delicacy and finesse to Champagne, two black grapes also used – the Pinot Noir and the Pinot Meunier. These give body and balance to the wine. When the wine is made solely from the Chardonnay grape it is known as Blanc de Blancs (white of whites). The resulting wine is very light, refreshing and delicate. If made only from black grapes it is called Blanc de Noirs and results in a much fuller, rounded, heavier Champagne. The great majority of Champagne is made from a combinatin of all three grapes which provides the beautiful unique balance that we all appreciate.

Most vineyards have a predominance of chalky soil which readily absorbs moisture to keep vine roots healthy. They are graded from 100 per cent (grands crus) to 80 per cent (premiers crus) with relative prices for the grapes per kilo at harvest time. Thus a grower with a 100 per cent graded vineyard can sell his grapes for 100 per cent of the price set by the main Champagne governing body (the CIVC).

Making Champagne

The grapes are carefully picked (*l'épluchage*) and any unworthies are discarded. The great Champagne houses use only the juice from the first pressing of the grapes, known as *vin de cuvée*. When the juice becomes wine it is tasted and a *cuvée* (blend) is made incorporating the special attributes of wines from different vineyards. It was Dom Pérignon (1638–1715) a Bénédictine monk and cellar master at the Abbey of Hautvillers near Épernay who first recognised the need for compensatory blending in order to make a balanced and consistent wine. He was also the first to introduce the cork as the stopper in Champagne bottles. Previously hemp stoppers soaked in oil were used, but, of course, these were never successful in keeping the sparkle in the bottle.

Once the cuvée or blend is agreed a sugar solution and yeast (*liqueur de tirage*) is added. The wine is bottled and a crown cap or temporary cork, held in position by a clamp (*agrafe*), is fitted. The bottles are then taken to deep cellars (*caves*) where they are laid on their sides. A second fermentation takes place and, as the bubbles cannot escape, the CO_2 becomes chemically bonded in the wine, resulting in sparkling wine. This second fermentation is known locally as 'Prise de Mousse', capturing the sparkle. The wine is then left undisturbed to mature for two or more years.

Before the wine can be sold, any sediment remaining in the bottle from the second fermentation has to be removed. The bottles are placed in a wooden frame called a *pupître* which can hold them in positions from the horizontal to the perpendicular. From time to time

Fig. 5.6 The remuage process

Fig. 5.7 Sediment collecting in neck of bottle

the cellar workman (*remueur*) twists and tilts each bottle, encouraging the sediment to slide from the body into the neck of the bottle. This operation known as *remuage* is completed in about 90 days and the trend is towards the mechanisation of this process using gyropalettes. The bottles, neck downwards, are then placed in a tank of freezing brine so that, when the cork or crown cap is removed, the frozen sediment pops out in the form of a pellet of ice (*dégorgement à la glace*), leaving behind beautifully clear sparkling and absolutely dry wine. The small amount of wine that is lost is made up with a Champagne and sugar solution known as *liqueur d'expédition* (shipping dosage). The sweetness of the liqueur d'expédition depends on the country for which the wine is destined and affects the wine's style. In fact when talking about the percentage of sugar in a bottle of Champagne, this refers only to that in the liqueur d'expédition. The addition of sugar, as it affects the sweetness of the wine, is indicated on the label (*see* below).

The bottles now get their second and final corks plus metal caps which are held firmly together by a wire muzzle or cage. Each bottle is dressed with foil and a neck and body label.

Name	Sugar in dosage
Ultra brut Brut de Brut Brut absolut Dosage zero }	None
Nature	
Brut	Up to 1 per cent
Extra sec, extra dry	1–2 per cent
Sec	2–4 per cent
Demi-sec	4–6 per cent
Demi-doux	6–8 per cent
Doux	8 per cent upwards

Champagne bottle names and sizes

Name	Metric	Imperial
Quarter-bottle	20 cl	6.0 fl oz
Half-bottle	37.5 cl	12.7 fl oz
Bottle	75 cl	25.4 fl oz
Magnum (2 bottles)	1.5 litres	50.7 fl oz
Jeroboam (double magnum) (4 bottles)	3 litres	101.4 fl oz
Rehoboam (6 bottles)	4.5 litres	152.1 fl oz
Methuselah (methusalem) (8 bottles)	6 litres	202.8 fl oz
Salmanazar (12 bottles)	9 litres	304.2 fl oz
Balthazar (16 bottles)	12 litres	405.6 fl oz
Nebuchadnezzar (20 bottles)	15 litres	507.1 fl oz

Styles of Champagne

Luxury Cuvée
Made by some firms in a really outstanding year and kept aside and nurtured through every stage of its development. These Champagnes are presented in beautifully elegant bottles sometimes decorated to mark a special occasion. Have your credit card ready as they are greatly expensive, but such wine is worthy of that really special occasion.

Examples are:

Dom Pérignon	Tattinger Comtes de Champagne
Dom Ruinart	Pol Roger Winston Churchill
Roderer Cristal	

Vintage Champagne
This is a wine from a single good year (it is, however, permissible to add up to 20 per cent of a wine from another specific year to assist the blend). Vintage wine will show the year on the label

Non-vintage Champagne
This is a blend of wines from different years which, for real value, is perhaps the best buy.

Pink Champagne
Available as vintage or non-vintage and made by leaving the grape skins with the must until the juice becomes pink in colour. It can also be made more simply by blending together red and white wines.

Grandes Marques Champagnes
Certain houses hold this distinction because they consistently produce excellent high-quality Champagne.

Ayala	G H Mumm
Bollinger	Perrier Jouët
Canard Duchêne	Piper Heidsieck
Clicquot Ponsardin	Pol Roger
Heidsieck Monopole	Pommery & Greno
Krug	Louis Roederer
Lanson	Ruinart
Moët & Chandon	Tattinger

Buyer's Own Brand (BOB)
Some firms will make a Champagne for a restaurant or a chain of restaurants that will be sold under the buyer's own label.

Recently Disgorged (Récemment Dégorgé) (RD)
These are special wines left to mature with their sediment in bottle for many years to produce a fine, full-flavoured, balanced wine. They are usually released for sale after about 8 to 10 years, but can remain healthy for much longer.

From 1994 other sparkling wines may not have, by law, the term Champagne method or méthode Champenoise ascribed to them to indicate their method of production. Instead, méthode traditionnelle or some other appropriate term will be substituted.

Corsica

Corsica, the largest of France's islands produces good red and white table wine, some of which has recently received the Vin de Corse Appellation Contrôlée distinction. The red Patrimonio is well acclaimed, as is the white Vin de Corse Porto-Vecchio. A feature of Corsican wine is its high alcohol content. Cap Corse is a rusty red, medium sweet, wine-based apéritif that is popular on the island.

Jura and Savoie

Jura

In the districts of Arbois, Côtes du Jura and L'Etoile red, white and rosé (*vinsgris*) wines are made. Many are sold under the Arbois appellation. Arbois is also famous for being the birthplace of Louis Pasteur, the great French scientist who, in 1857, proved that fermentation was a physiological process, when he explained scientifically the process of vinous fermentation. Some unique wines are also made in the Jura such as Vin Jaune (yellow wine), Vin de Paille (straw wine) and Macvin.

Vin Jaune
This wine, made from Savagnin grapes, is a wine after the style of fino sherry. The grapes are picked late, often in December, and the cold weather induces a slow fermentation. As the wine matures in cask (sometimes for as long as eight years) a yeast mould (*flor*) develops on the surface of the wine. This imparts an austere dryness and hazelnut flavour to the pale, golden wine which has an alcohol strength of 15 per cent. A good example, Château Chalon, is traditionally sold in a dumpy bottle called a *clavelin*.

Vin de Paille

This dessert wine gets its name from the fact that the grapes are laid out on straw (*paille*) to dry and partially shrink them before pressing. Sometimes the grapes are hung from rafters during the winter to concentrate the juice. The finished wine has a flavour of quinces.

Macvin

This apéritif wine, is fairly similar to white port, and is fortified with local *eau-de-vie-de-marc* and flavoured with ingredients such as coriander and cinnamon. It is best served chilled and is also nice with ice.

Côtes du Jura Mousseux is the finest of the sparkling wine appellations.

Savoie

Savoie is situated between Lyon and Geneva. The area is noted for its still and sparkling white wine. Best whites are Crépy, Apremont, Seyssel, Roussette de Savoie and the sparkling wine Royal Seyssel made by Varichon and Clerc. The reds, often made from the Gamay and Pinot Noir grapes, are best exemplified by the Cruët and Motmélian styles.

Loire

The lovely Loire valley wines are much sought after today, be they produced by a co-operative or domaine bottled from a single vineyard. Red, white, rosé and sparkling wines are produced. The reds and better rosés are made from the Cabernet Franc grape and the whites from Sauvignon Blanc, Chenin Blanc, Muscadet and Chasselas grapes. Although the wines may never be considered great, they are always good and present fair value in these days of upwardly mobile prices.

The Loire can be divided into four main wine-growing districts: Central Loire (around Sancerre, Pouilly Fumé, Pouilly-sur-Loire, Quincy and Reuilly), Touraine (incorporating Tours, Bougueil, Chinon and Blois), Anjou (including Angers and Saumur) and the Pays Nantais near the Atlantic coast. The best dry whites are Muscadet, Sancerre and Pouilly Blanc Fumé.

LOIRE

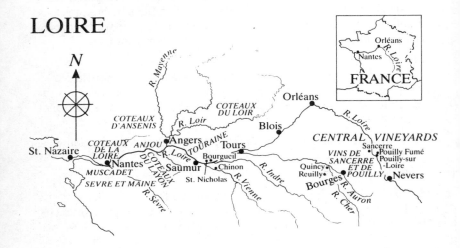

Fig. 5.8 Loire wine-producing areas

Muscadet

Made from the Muscadet (Melon de Bourgogne) grape around the city of Nantes, this is a fresh dry wine with an attractive acidity. It is ideal as an apéritif, and goes extremely well with shellfish. The most popular style is Muscadet *sur lie*. The wine is left to mature in cask on its lees before bottling, which imparts freshness, depth of flavour and an intense bouquet.

Sancerre

While some red Sancerre from the Pinot Noir grape is available, the wine we have come to know as Sancerre is a delightful, dry, smoky white wine. It is produced in the Cher Department in Central Loire and can be drunk young, but it improves with bottle age.

Pouilly Blanc Fumé

A wine quite similar to Sancerre, but with a little more brightness and elegance. It gets its Fumé appendage not only because of its gun flint flavour, but also because of the smoky, blue, dust haze reflected by the ripe grapes over the vineyards around Pouilly-sur-Loire in the cooler autumn air.

Other Loire wines

The medium dry white wines of the Loire are Vouvray and Saumur. Vouvray, from near Tours in Touraine, is especially popular because of its versatility and genuine and agreeable nature. Saumur as a still wine is more difficult to obtain outside France. However, it is well marketed as a classical method sparkling wine, as is Vouvray sometimes. It is produced in the district around Saumur, in the Anjou region of the Loire. Both Vouvray and Saumur are always pleasing to taste.

Quarts de Chaume and Bonnezeaux are two of the better sweet white wines from the Coteaux du Layon area in Anjou. Made in the style of Sauternes, they improve as they mature. The rosé wines of Anjou are very popular and those sold as Cabernet d'Anjou are of superior quality. Of the reds, Chinon, Bourgueil, Saint-Nicolas-de-Bourgueil and Saumur Champigny are bright and fruity with a good depth of flavour. Try them slightly chilled.

The Midi

Languedoc and Roussillon produce everyday quaffing wines. It is estimated that up to 40 per cent of France's total production is made here. That is why the region is popularly known as the belly of France, because it makes huge amounts of inexpensive table wines to which the French themselves are very partial in bars, cafés and at home. While some of the wine is used as a base in the production of vermouth, the best quality (mostly red) is sold simply as Coteaux de Languedoc, Roussillon, Corbières, Fitou, Minervois and Costières du Gard.

The real stars of this wine lake are the *vins doux naturels*. Made mostly from the Muscat grape and sometimes from the Grenache, the fermentation is stopped and the sweetness retained by adding alcohol to the fermenting must. The finished wines have an alcohol content of 17 per cent. The best examples are Grand Roussillon, Muscat de Frontignan, Muscat de Rivesaltes and the red Banyuls.

A quite outstanding dry sparkling wine, Blanquette de Limoux, is

also made. Seriously considered as the best effervescent wine outside
Champagne, it has elegance and fragrance and is at its most refreshing when drunk young.

The best dry white table wines are Clairette du Languedoc, Clairette
de Bellegarde from Gard, and Picpoul de Pinet from Hérault. Around
Montpellier, great quantities of red, white and rosé wines, known as
Vins Sables du Golfe du Lion, are produced. The vines are mostly cul-
tivated in sand dunes and in the sandy marshes close to the
Camargue. The area is especially noted for the largest single vineyard
in France – Domaines des Salins du Midi – whose wines are marketed
under the brand name Listel. Perhaps the most interesting of these is
Listel Gris de Gris, a blush wine, made from free-run juice of the
Grenache and Cinsault grapes.

Provence

Provence wines are generally sold in unusually shaped bottles with
distinctive, almost lavish, labels. Those who have drunk these wines
in the South of France will know they go wonderfully well with the
foods and the atmosphere of the Mediterranean. Take them away
from the sea and sunshine, they seem a little jaded, but perhaps it is
all in the mind. Red, white and rosé wines are produced almost every-
where. The red and rosés are from the Cinsault, Cabernet Sauvignon,
Grenache and Mourvèdre grapes and the whites from the Ugni Blanc,
Clairette and Macabéo, Marsanne, Rolle, and Sauvignon Blanc.

The wines

The main wine-growing regions of Provence are around Bandol,
Bellet, Cassis, Côtes de Provence and Palette.

Bandol
Red, white and rosé wines are produced. The reds age well, whereas
the rosés are ready for drinking within a few months. The whites,
though scarce (about 6 per cent of the total crop), are dry and spicy.
All are fairly expensive.

Bellet
Again red, white and rosé wines are made. They are rarely seen outside France as most are drunk locally in the restaurants and cafés in
and around Nice.

Cassis
Red, white and rosé wines are produced, although white is predominant in quality and availability.

Côtes de Provence
Many Provence wines are sold under this label as well as under Aix en Provence. The rosés seem to be the best, the reds are improving, but the whites lack zip and zing.

Palette
This area, near Aix-en-Provence, makes good red wines and decent white and rosé wines, though not in considerable quantities.

Rhône

The Rhône vineyards stretch from Lyon to Avignon (*see* page 96) producing red, white and rosé wines of class. The reds are the real heavyweights: big, masculine wines, strong in alcohol and flavour. They are usually made from the Syrah grape or from a combination of Grenache, Cinsault, Carignan, Mourvèdre and others. In fact there are 13 varities that are permitted to be used in the making of the famous Châteauneuf-du-Pape. The outstanding reds, besides the spicy Châteauneuf, are Côte Rôtie, Hermitage, Crozes-Hermitage, Saint-Josèph, Cornas, Gigondas, Lirac, Côtes du Rhône Villages and Côtes du Ventoux.

The best whites are Château Grillet and Condrieu made from the Viognier grape. Other white grape varieties are Rousanne, Marsanne, Clairette and Ugni Blanc. Tavel is France's best rosé wine and is made predominantly from the Grenache grape. Saint-Péray is a clean, lively, sparkling wine made by the classical method, as is the better-known Clairette de Die which can also be demi-sec or doux. The great vin doux naturel is Muscat de Beaumes-de-Venise which is fortified with grape brandy during fermentation to preserve its sweetness.

South-West France

The main wine-producing regions in South-West France are Bergerac, Cahors, Gaillac, Jurançon, Irouléguy and Madiran.

RHÔNE

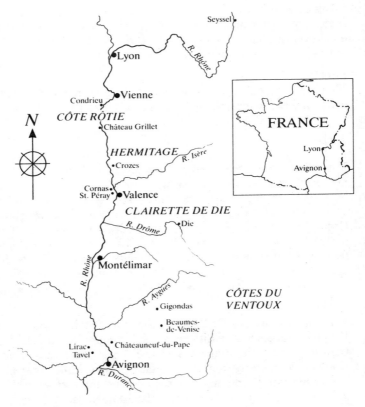

Fig. 5.9 Rhône wine-producing areas

Bergerac

Bergerac vineyards are located on both banks of the Dordogne where the Dordogne Valley begins. The wines are red, white and rosé, but the outstanding wine of the region is the deep golden, luscious, creamy rich Monbazillac made, like Sauternes, from grapes affected by the *Botrytis cinerea* fungus. Next best are the dry reds Bergerac, Côte de Bergerac and Pécharmant.

Cahors

This town on the River Lot is famous for its dark red wines made from Malbec or Cot grapes. In youth the wines are exceptionally robust, but usually they are allowed to age for years in cask to provide the finesse which has made them so popular in France. The aged wines are very good, but very expensive.

Gaillac

Gaillac is best known for its white wine made from Mauzac grapes. Some of the wine is *perlé* (slightly sparkling). The rosé and red wines are usually made from Gamay grapes and are mostly drunk locally.

Jurançon

The wine growers on the foothills of the Pyrenees, to the south and west of Pau, make mainly red and dry white wines nowadays. Some of the traditional sweet white wine called Jurançon Moelleux is still around, but it is expensive for what it is.

Irouléguy

Red, white and rosé wines are made on the western side of the Atlantic Pyrenees on the Spanish border. Although they are typical *'vins de vacances'*, the best reds are now available in Britain.

Madiran

Produces mostly red wines made almost exclusively from local Tannat grapes. This deep-coloured, distinctive wine is a great favourite in the Pyrenees.

───────── Germany ─────────

German wines are rightly popular because they are easy to drink, can be drunk on their own as a conversation wine (*Unterhaltungswein*) or with a wide variety of foods. Overlooking some recent indiscretions they are consistently well made and have a reputation for reliability at all levels. Their fruity flavour, low alcohol, attractive balance of acid and sugar and reasonable price have particular appeal to new wine drinkers, which is one of the reasons why Liebfraumilch, for example, is the biggest selling white table wine in Britain today. However, it should be noted that Liebfraumilch can only ever be a QbA wine (page 100) and can never be regarded as a classic or even fine wine as it is a blended wine from either the Pfalz, Rheinhessen, Nahe or Rheingau regions. Even so, there are hundreds and thousands

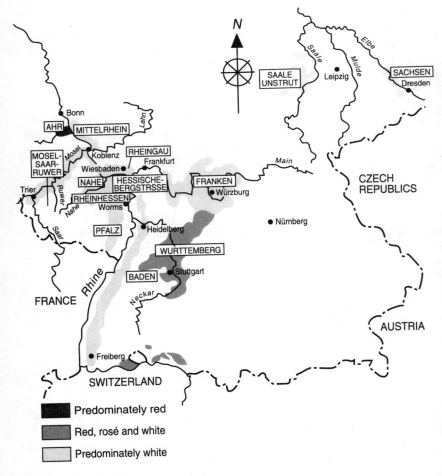

Fig. 5.10 Wine-producing regions of Germany

of people who are happy with it. To prove the point, next time you go to a 'cash wine' banquet take a look at the bottles around you.

Eighty-eight per cent of German wines are white. The rest are red and rosé (Schillerwein) wines. Although they are often sold under a proprietary or brand label many are identified by their region, district or vineyard and by the degree of grape ripeness at harvest time. Sometimes when the grapes have not fully ripened, beet or cane sugar is added to the unfermented must in order to raise the alcohol level during fermentation up to that of a similar wine of a good year. This practice is called *Verbesserung* (chaptalisation in France) which 'improves' the alcohol content but not the quality. The resulting wines may not be sold as vintage wines and only the classifications of Deutscher Tafelwein, Deutscher Landwein and Qualitätswein bestimmter Anbaugebiete wines may be 'improved' in this manner.

The category Qualitätswein mit Prädikat, which is the top tier of German wines, may not by law be so improved. Of course with some of the lesser wines the art of the cellar master can produce a variety of styles of wine from the same basic dry wine. This is achieved by adding *Süssreserve* (sweet reserve – unfermented, sterile grape juice) to the finished wine just before bottling.

The two major categories, which are also subdivided, are *Tafelwein* (table wine) and *Qualitätswein* (quality wine).

Tafelwein

Deutscher Tafelwein (German table wine)

This is a basic German wine made only from German-grown grapes. There is also a simple Tafelwein which is made from a combination of grapes from both Germany and the EU.

Deutscher Landwein (German regional wine)

This is a superior Tafelwein in that it has more character and is made from grapes grown in any one of the 20 designated Landwein regions.

Qualitätswein

Qualitätswein bestimmter Anbaugebiete (QbA)

(Quality wine from designated regions) Wines in this category may be dry or slightly sweet. They are usually made from fully ripe grapes but, like the Deutscher Tafelwein and Landwein, the grape juice is frequently improved (Verbesserung) through the addition of sugar to raise the alcohol content – similar to the French chaptalisation.

Qualitätswein mit Prädikat (QmP)

(Quality wine with distinction) These are completely natural wines made from fully ripe and overripe grapes. There are six levels of quality (no sugaring of the must is allowed):

1 Kabinett
This gets its name from the fact that the wine is good enough to be kept in the winegrower's own cabinet (but he has let you have it instead). It is fruity, light and dry and completely genuine.

2 Spätlese (late harvested)
Spätlese wine is made from grapes picked about a week after the normal harvest. These riper grapes make fuller, sweeter wine.

3 Auslese (selected harvesting)
Made from selected bunches of late-harvested grapes, these wines are even sweeter, fuller and stay longer on the palate, than Spätlese wines.

4 Beerenauslese BA (selective picked grapes)
This wine is made from individually picked grapes which, because of their overripeness, have begun to shrivel on the vine. The resulting wine is very rich (which you must also be to buy it!).

5 Eiswein (ice wine)
Eiswein was first introduced in 1842 and made from overripe grapes which have been frozen by severe frosts. The grapes are picked and pressed at a maximum of –6°C. The grape juice is very concentrated and must have a minimum sugar content equal, at least, to a Beerenauslese. These wines are not made every year and can be made only when the correct conditions prevail. Although they are very sweet indeed they are not sticky or cloying as they have a welcome balance of tartness.

6 Trockenbeerenauslese TBA (selectively picked raisined grapes)
This is made from shrivelled raisin-like grapes which have been
affected by *Edelfäule (Botrytis cinerea)* fungus. The grapes are individually picked in this prime condition and the vineyards are gone
over time and time again until the harvest is over. The Edelfäule
punctures the skins of the grapes, then, as the water content
evaporates the grape sugars and acids become concentrated and the
resulting grape syrup, when fermented and matured, tastes like nectar.

Deutscher Sekt, the sparkling wine of Germany, is made in
all the wine regions. Since 1986 it must be made only from
German wine. The best is made by the méthode traditionnelle (Champagne method) and is very much quality con-
trolled. It is categorised as Qualitätsschaumweine bA, or
Sekt bA, and must come from a designated region.
Sparkling wine is also made by the closed tank (*charmat*)
method and is known locally as Grossraumgarverwahren
Schaumwein. There are other wines with some sparkle and
these are known as Perlwein or Spritzig, similar to the
pétillant wines of France.
Really good examples of quality Sekt are Deinhard's Lila
Imperial, Fürst von Metternich, Reichsrat von Buhl Riesling
Extra Brut and Deutz & Geldermann Brut.

Appellation of origin

Germany has 13 specified wine-growing *Gebiete* (regions) (e.g. Mosel-
Saar-Ruwer) which, within them, contain the 39 *Bereiche* (districts),
the name of which is usually taken from the best-known village of the
district (e.g. Bernkastel). This is further broken down into 161
Grosslagen (sub-district or collective vineyard sites, e.g. Bernkasteler
Badstube) and 2,644 *Einzellagen* (individual vineyard sites, e.g.
Bernkasteler Doktor).

Label language

Once you understand the terminology, German wine labels are very
informative and easy to understand. The label should reveal:

1 Wine category – whether it is a:
   (a) Deutscher Tafelwein – an ordinary wine made entirely from German grapes;
   (b) Landwein – which can come from any of 20 specified regions;
   (c) Gebiet (region) – wine made in a particular region;
   (d) Bereich – wine made in a sub-region;
   (e) Grosslage – wine made in a particular district or collective vineyard site;
   (f) Gemeinde – wine made in a village in a district;
   (g) Einzellage – wine made in an individual vineyard.
2 The vineyard name will be preceded by the village name in possessive form carrying the suffix '-er'.
3 Vintage year – the year the wine is made.
4 Grape variety – Riesling, Silvaner, etc. from which the wine was made.
5 Taste of the wine; *Trocken* (dry), *Halb Trocken* (less dry), *Diabetikerwein* (suitable for diabetics).
6 QbA – quality wine from designated regions.
7 QmP – the distinction of the wine and manner of harvesting (e.g. Spätlese, Auslese, etc).

Fig. 5.11 German wine label.

8 Amtliche Prüfungsnummer (AP number) – the official testing number indicating that the wine has passed an official chemical and sensory test. The last two digits reveal the year the bottler made the application for his wine to be tested.

9 Erzeugerabfüllung – estate bottled or Aus eigenem Lesegut (from the producer's own vineyard).

Grapes

Up to 50 different grapes species are grown in German vineyards, many of them new or experimental. The grape variety does not have to appear on a label but, when it does, there is a guarantee that at least 85 per cent of the wine has been produced from the indicated grape. About 87 per cent of the vineyards are planted with white grape varieties, the remainder being black grapes. The wine styles produced are:

- white wine
- sparkling white wine (known as Sekt)
- rosé wine (Weissherbst) made from black grapes only
- Rotling wine from a combination of white and black grapes resulting in such specialities as Rotgold in Baden and Schillerwein in Württemberg
- red wine

The three noble grapes are Riesling, Silvaner and Müller-Thurgau:

Riesling	accounts for about 21 per cent of the crop and is the undisputed quality leader producing Germany's finest wines, elegant, well-balanced and full of flavour
Silvaner	accounts for about 8 per cent of the crop and makes softer more gentle wines which are best drunk in their youth
Müller-Thurgau	accounts for 24 per cent of the crop and is a cross between the Riesling and Silvaner vines. This hybrid yields good crops, is sturdy and withstands vine diseases well, producing mildly acetic, fruity wines with a pronounced flowery bouquet. It was first developed by a Professor Müller from Thurgau (Switzerland) in 1882

Other white wine grapes are Kerner (a cross between the Riesling and the red Trollinger grapes), Elbling, Ruländer, Gewürztraminer, Gutedel, Scheurebe, Ortega, Morio-Muskat and Bacchus. The black grapes include Trollinger (originally from the Tyrol), Portugieser (originating in Austria) and Spätburgunder (Pinot Noir).

Wine-growing areas

The 13 specified wine-growing areas are located near or on the banks of rivers:

- Baden, Hessische Bergstrasse, Mittelrhein, Rheingau, Rheinhessen and Pfalz are all on or near the banks of the Rhine
- Franken is on the Main
- Württemberg is on the banks of the Neckar
- Mosel-Saar-Ruwer, Ahr, Nahe and Saale-Unstrut are all named after their rivers
- Sachsen vineyards are on the banks of the Elbe.

The regions (listed alphabetically), together with examples of their better-known villages and vineyards, are given below.

Ahr

This very small region has the most northerly vineyards in Germany. The vineyards are mostly located on steep hillsides and follow the river as it flows into the Rhine, south of Bonn. The majority of the wine produced is red from the Spätburgunder and Portugieser grapes and varies from velvet-smooth to light and ordinary. The Riesling and Müller-Thurgau grapes make lively refreshing white wines. Despite their location many of the reds are on the sweet side and, like the whites, are best drunk in their own locality.

Village	Vineyard
Heimersheim	Heimersheimer Landskrone
Neuenahr	Neuenahrer Sonnenberg
Walporzheim	Walporzheimer Gärkammer

Baden

This longish, narrow stretch of vineyards is the most southerly of all the German regions. The vineyards are located between Heidelberg and Bodensee, real Black Forest country. Riesling, Müller-Thurgau, Ruländer, Gutedel and Gewürztraminer grapes produce a variety of white wines, some fragrant and fresh, others spicy and full of aroma. The Spätburgunder grapes are used to make full-bodied, smooth red wines and the popular rosé known as Weissherbst (in reality a white wine with red tinges).

Village	Vineyard
Michelfeld	Michelfelder Himmelberg
Zulzfeld	Burg Ravensburger
Durbach	Durchbacher Schlossberg

Franken

This most easterly of the German regions has Müller-Thurgau and the Silvaner vines growing along the hillsides overlooking the River Main and its tributaries. The wines, which are mostly white, are also known as *Steinwein* because they are stone dry in character. They are sold in beautifully labelled, green, squat, flagon-shaped bottles known as *Bocksbeutel*.

Village	Vineyard
Castell	Casteller Kirchberg
Iphofen	Iphofener Julius-Echter-Berg
	Iphofener Kalb
Würzburg	Würzburger Innere Leiste
	Würzburger Stein

Hessische Bergstrasse

This small region lies between Darmstadt and Heidelberg on the east bank of the Rhine. The farmers mostly sell their grapes (mainly

Riesling, Silvaner and Müller-Thurgau) to the co-operatives (*Winzergenossenschaften*) who make a pleasing white wine, generally for local consumption.

Village	Vineyard
Bensheim	Bensheimer Streichling
Heppenheim	Heppenheimer Centegericht

Mittelrhein

This beautiful region stretches south of Bonn for about 95 km (60 miles) and the terraced vineyards have their hillside homes on both banks of the river Rhine. Mainly a white wine region, with the Riesling, Müller-Thurgau and the Kerner grapes giving lively, fruity and flavoursome wines.

Village	Vineyard
Oberwesel	Oberweseler St Martinsberg
Boppard Hamm	Bopparder Hamm Ohlenberg
Kaub	Kauber Backofen
Bacharach	Bacharacher Posten

Mosel-Saar-Ruwer

It is in this region that the classy wines begin, with the Riesling grape dominating. The vineyards are located on precariously steep, slatey slopes which present a severe challenge to the grape harvesters at vintage time. Since the vineyards are so widespread, the wines vary in style according to location but, at their best, they have a freshness, delicacy of flavour and lovely bouquet.

Village	Vineyard
Bernkastel-Kues	Bernkasteler Doktor
	Bernkasteler Schlossberg
Enkirch	Enkircher Steffensberg

Erden	Erdener Prälat
	Erdener Treppchen
Graach	Graacher Himmelreich
	Graacher Josephshöfer
Kasel	Kaseler Hitzlay
	Kaseler Nieschen
Ockfen	Ockfener Bockstein
	Ockfener Herrenberg
Piesport	Piesporter Goldtröpfchen
	Piesporter Gunterslay
Wehlen	Wehlener Sonnenuhr
Zell	Zeller Dommherrenberg

Nahe

The vineyards are mostly found on the steep slopes along the River Nahe and its tributaries. The Müller-Thurgau, Silvaner and the Riesling grapes produce wines which are light and have an attractive, sublte crispness.

Village	Vineyard
Bad Kreuznach	Kreuznacher Brückes
	Kreuznacher Narrenkappe
Munster	Munsterer Dautenpflänzer
	Munsterer Pittersberg
Niederhausen	Niederhausener Hermannsberg
Schlossböckelheim	Schlossböckelheimer Felsenberg
	Schlossböckelheimer Kupfergrube

Pfalz

This region has almost 80 km (50 miles) of uninterrupted vineyards and produces more wine than any other region in Germany. The main grapes used are the Riesling, Müller-Thurgau, Silvaner, Kerner and Morio-Muskat, producing the typical, rich, spicy, aromatic white wines. The Portugieser grape makes good smooth fruity red wines.

The region is also known as the Palatinate after the word *Pfalz* (a derivation of the word *palast* or *palace*, which came originally from the Latin *palatium*).

Village	Vineyard
Bad Dürkheim	Dürkheimer Fuchsmantel
	Dürkheimer Spielberg
Deidesheim	Deidesheimer Hohenmorgen
	Deidesheimer Leinhöhle
Forst	Forster Jesuitengarten
	Forster Musenhang
Kallstadt	Kallstadter Annaberg
	Kallstadter Steinacker

Rheingau

Regarded as the classic wine region in Germany, Rheingau stretches from Hochheim on the River Main to Lorch close to the Mittelrhein. Most of the vineyards are situated on picturesque hillsides, with forests, castles and cloisters interspersing, making a wonderful panorama of beauty and serenity. The Riesling grape dominates, producing wines to match the scenery – distinctive and elegant, at once both gentle and domineering. The best reds of Germany are also made here particularly at Assmannshausen from the noble Spätburgunder grape.

The really great wines from this region are sold by the vineyard label and are estate bottled.

Village	Vineyard
Assmannshausen	Assmannshauser Höllenberg
Erbach	Erbacher Marcobrunn
	Erbacher Michelmark
Geisenheim	Geisenheimer Kläuserweg
	Geisenheimer Rothenberg
Hallgarten	Hallgartener Schönhell
Hattenheim	Hattenheimer Nussbrunnen
	Hattenheimer Wisselbrunnen
Hochheim	Hochheimer Domdechaney
	Hochheimer Kirchenstück
Johannisberg	Johannisberger Hölle
	Schloss Johannisberg

Oestrich	Oestricher Doosberg
	Schloss Reichhartshausen
Rauenthal	Rauenthaler Baiken
Rüdesheim	Rüdesheimer Berg Rottland
	Rüdesheimer Berg Schlossberg
Winkel	Schloss Vollrads

> The wines from the village of Hochheim were favourites of Queen Victoria and became popularly known as Hocks. Indeed there is a single vineyard named after her called Hochheimer Königin Victoria Berg.

Rheinhessen

This is the largest wine-producing region in Germany, covering an area 30 km by 50 km (20 miles by 30 miles) and lying in a valley overlooked by rolling hills, with some slopes under the vine. The area is the birthplace and the original home of Liebfraumilch – formerly made only in vineyards surrounding the Church of Our Lady (Liebfrauenkirche) in the town of Worms.

Although the area is huge by German standards, in terms of overall production, it still produces less wine than the Pfalz. The grapes, mainly Riesling, Müller-Thurgau and Silvaner, produce the soft, mild, medium-bodied white wines for which the region is famous. The Portugieser and the Spätburgunder grapes make smooth full-bodied red wines.

Village	Vineyard
Bingen	Binger Scharlachberg
Oppenheim	Oppenheimer Kreuz
	Oppenheimer Sackträger
Nierstein	Niersteiner Orbel
	Niersteiner Hipping

Saale-Unstrut

The Müller-Thurgau, Silvaner, Bacchus and Riesling vines are grown on small terraces along the course of the Saale and Unstrut Rivers producing light, soft, flowery, dry white wines. A little red wine is also made from the Portugieser grapes.

Village	Vineyard
Freyburg	Weingut Decker
	Weingut Pawis
Bad Kösen	Weingut Lützkendorf

Sachsen

These vineyards are sited along the Elbe River between Pillnitz and Diesbar. The Müller-Thurgau, Weissburgunder, Traminer, Gutedel, Riesling and Ruländer vines are grown on very steep terraces producing dry, white wines with fruity acidity. Elbtal Sekt is a local speciality sparkler.

Village	Vineyard
Meissen	Weingut Proschwitz
Radebeul	Weingut Klaus Seifert
Diesbar	Weinbau Jan Ulrich

Württemberg

This region produces an abundance of red, white and rosé wines. Rosés are called *Schillerwein* (shimmering wines) because of their bright and breezy personality.

This region has its vineyards mainly on the banks of the River Neckar. It is Germany's largest producer of red wines, all of which are hearty and fulsome, coming from the Spätburgunder, Portugieser, Trollinger, Müllerrebe and Lemberger grapes. The white wines are fruity and have a distinctive earthy flavour. The commercial centre is Stuttgart and not much of the wine is allowed to leave the region. (There is a huge thirst locally!)

Village	Vineyard
Gundelsheim	Gundelsheimer Himmelreich
Maulbronn	Maulbronner Eilfingerberg
Weikersheim	Weikersheimer Schmecker

Greece

In contrast to the wines of Cyprus, Greek wines tend to be somewhat parochial, flat and not very exciting. Best known is the famous, or infamous, Retsina which is flavoured with pine-tree resin obtained from Aleppo pines in Attica. This imparts a slight turpentine flavour which many people find pleasant to taste especially with spicy foods. It is white or pink in colour and Metaxa's Retsina is a style of note.

The dry white wines Demestica, Santa Helena, Antika and Pallini are light and pleasant, either as apéritifs or as accompaniments to light food. Demestica also appears as a red wine and the red Château Carras and the dark, fruity Naoussa are fast establishing good reputations. Two sweet wines, the deep golden Muscat of Samos and the intense red port-like Mavrodaphne, are popular dessert wines.

Hungary

Hungarian wines are usually named after the district in which they have been made and are marketed for export by the state monopoly called Monimpex. The reds are big and burly, good foils for the heavily flavoured food. The whites are also full of personality, for the same reason.

The best known of all the wines is Tokay Aszú, a luscious golden wine produced from the Furmint and Hárslevelü grapes. Heat and dampness encourage the mould *Botrytis cinerea* (noble rot) to form on the skins. These shrink, and the grape juice becomes very concentrated as the water content is reduced and the glycerine content increases. The grapes are collected in *puttonyos* (hods) – smallish wooden barrels containing about 30 litres (8 gallons). They are then crushed to a pasty mass and added to new must as it ferments in a standard vat. The more puttonyos added, the sweeter the eventual wine. The number added will be shown on the label as either three, four or five puttonyos.

Another style of wine that used to be made is Tokay Essenz which was produced from the syrupy juice which trickled from the grapes as they lay waiting in the tubs to be pressed. The resulting grape essence is not now made into wine for the commercial market, but is added to the Aszú style to enhance the product.

Many of the white table wines are sold simply as Hungarian Riesling or Balatoni Riesling but others are named: Badacsony, Mór, Somló, Pécs and Mecsek, usually with the grape appendage Riesling or Furmint. Of the reds Egri Bikavér (Bull's Blood) is the most celebrated, but Kadarka, Vilány, Sopron and the ones labelled Hungarian Merlot are good-value wines.

Israel

Jewish interest in wine making goes back to the time of Moses and is acknowledged throughout the Old Testament. The Société Coopérative Vigneronne des Grandes Caves is the major producer of wine in Israel accounting for 75 per cent of the output. It markets its wines under the brand name Carmel. The modern wine industry was founded in the 1880s by Baron Edmond de Rothschild. He planted vineyards and established wineries which he later generously donated to the growers. Much of the wine is Kosher, made under Rabbinical supervision, and the main export market is to the United States. In 1957 the Israeli Wine Institute was formed at Rehovat, and since then there has been a gradual improvement in all aspects of wine making. The wines range from dry to sweet, reds and whites, with some fortified and sparkling wines also made. Of the table wines, the white Carmel Hock, Château Montagne, Yarden Sauvignon Blanc and Palwin are of a good standard. The best reds are Gamla Cabernet Sauvignon, Château Windsor, Adom Atic, Yarden Cabernet Sauvignon, Yarden Merlot and Golan Cabernet Sauvignon.

Of the dessert wines, Yarden Late Harvested Sauvignon Blanc made from *Botrytis*-affected grapes is really fine. The better sparkling wines such as Yarden Brut, Yarden Blanc de Blancs and Gamla Rosé are made by the méthode traditionnelle.

KOSHER WINE

For a wine to be considered Kosher there are two basic requirements:

1 Only Kosher items may be used in the wine-making process;
2 Only religiously observant Jews may touch the product or equipment at the winery.

Nothing in the production affects wine quality. Traditional methods regarding fermentation, maturation, blending and bottling are adhered to.

Italy

The Italian wine growers once had a reputation for being careless makers of wine. Consequently they found difficulty in selling their wines abroad, except possibly to countries where immigrants from Italy had formed into sizeable communities. So, with little incentive to improve the product, the wines continued to languish, although much was used as a base for fortified and flavoured wines, spirits and liqueurs. An Act of Parliament was passed in 1963 aimed at improving the product just as the French wine laws did for French wines. However, many of the wine growers refused to be bridled by what they considered to be petty restrictions. Even today some of the very best producers operate outside the regulation laws and can now only describe their wines as table wines.

The ladder of quality

Vino da Tavola	(table wine) – the lowest grade, plonk by another name, although some so-called table wines may be of high quality
Vino da Tavolo con Indicazione Geografica	guarantees origin not quality

ITALY

1   VALLE D'AOSTA
2   PIEDMONT
3   LOMBARDY
4   TRENTINO-ALTO ADIGE
5   FRIULI-VENEZIA GIULIA
6   VENETO
7   LIGURIA
8   EMILIA ROMAGNA
9   TUSCANY
10 UMBRIA
11 THE MARCHES
12 LAZIO
13 ABRUZZI
14 CAMPANIA
15 MOLISE
16 PUGLIA
17 BASILICATA
18 CALABRIA
19 SICILY
20 SARDINIA

Fig. 5.12 Wine-producing regions of Italy

Denominazione di Origine Controllata	(DOC) – indicates that the wine was made from specific grapes grown in a specific area and made and matured according to the best local custom and practice. Guarantees the origin of the wine
Denominazione di Origine Controllata e Garantita	(DOCG) – is a newish top-tier classification which guarantees not only the origin but controls the type of grape, yield per hectare, minimum alcohol content, the method of viticulture and vinification. Furthermore, it guarantees that the wine has undergone a rigid chemical and sensory testing for quality and type. Only six wines originally merited this classification: reds – Chianti, Brunello di Montalcino and Vino Nobile di Montepulciano all produced in Tuscany,

Barolo and Barbaresco from Piedmont;
white – Albana di Romagna from Emilia-
Romagna

Debate goes on about whether the laws have helped to improve the
quality of Italian wine. Suffice is to say that the wines are on offer
worldwide today, some horrible stuff in screw-capped bottles and
some splendid stuff as well.

Label language

Abboccato	slightly sweet
Amabile	semi-sweet
Annata	vintage
Asciutto	bone dry
Azienda	estate
Bianco	white
Bottiglia	bottle
Cantina Sociale (Cooperativa)	winery run by a co-operative
Casa Vinicola	wine company
Chiaretto	deep rosé
Classico	classical or best part of a particular wine area (e.g. Chianti Classico)
Dolce	sweet
Frizzantino	slightly sparkling
Imbottigliato da	bottled by
Nero	dark red
Pradicato	control instigated by local wine growers; associated with *vino da tavola* when the wine has been produced from non-traditional grapes
Riserva	matured for a specific number of years
Riserva speciale	like Riserva but older
Rosato	rosé or pink wine
Rosso	red
Secco	dry
Spumante	foaming or sparkling

Spumante Classico	sparkling wine made by the Champagne method
Superiore	wines of superior quality with a good alcohol strength
Stravecchio	aged old wines
Vecchio	old
Vendemmia	harvest
Vino da Pasto	ordinary wine (vin ordinaire)

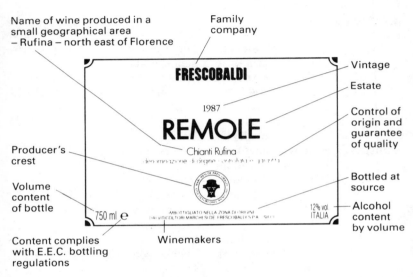

Name of wine produced in a small geographical area – Rufina – north east of Florence

Family company

Vintage

Estate

Control of origin and guarantee of quality

Producer's crest

Volume content of bottle

Bottled at source

Alcohol content by volume

Content complies with E.E.C. bottling regulations

Winemakers

Fig. 5.13 Italian wine label

Principal wine districts and wines

Piedmont

The home of vermouth which originated in Turin, the capital of Piedmont. This district is renowned for Italy's best-known sparkling wine, Asti Spumante – Asti being the town where it is made, *spumante* means foaming or sparkling. The best is made from the Muscat grape and by the Spumante Classico method (Champagne method). Cheaper varieties are produced by the charmat (closed tank) method. Two red wines, Barolo and Barbaresco, made from Nebbiolo grapes are really excellent, as is Barbera which is named after its own grape, and Gattinara.

Tuscany

This region is renowned for its red wines, Chianti Classico, Brunello di Montalcino and Vino Nobile di Montepulciano. Chianti has traditionally been made from the Sangiovese grape (although others are now permitted in the blend) and is usually sold in a globular shaped bottle (*fiasco*) which is partly covered with straw – not only for appearance but, more practically, to prevent the bottles breaking when carried *en masse*. Chianti Classico wines are nowadays more usually found in Bordeaux-style bottles which facilitates their laying down for slow maturation. Watch out for the black rooster neck label – this is a sign of quality. Furthermore the word *riserva* on a label implies that the wine has matured for five years in cask.

Trentino-Alto Adige

This region in the South Tyrol belonged to Austria until 1919 when it was ceded to Italy as a result of the Treaty of Saint Germain. This is mentioned because, even nowadays, the wines are marketed in both German and Italian. The wines from Alto Adige are first class. The sparkling Gran Spumante is second to none in Italy. Made by the Champagne method and from the Riesling and Pinot Bianco grapes, it is a real treat to drink and a pleasant discovery for those who think Italian spumante is nothing more than sparkling liquid sultanas. Of the whites, the Traminer Aromatico, Terlaner, Rhine Riesling and Pinot Bianco are all refreshing and good. The reds Lago di Caldaro, Santa Maddelena and Pinot Nero sell well, especially in Austria and Germany where they are very popular.

Umbria

The cathedral city of Orvieto gives its name to its most famous white wines – Orvieto Secco, which is dry, and Orvieto Abboccato or Amabile (meaning soft in the mouth) which is medium sweet. The red and white Torgiano are also important Umbrian wines.

The Marches

The dry white wines Verdicchio dei Castelli di Jesi and Verdicchio di Matelica are best here. Often sold in 'waisted' bottles, they have a pale straw colour and a slightly bitter aftertaste. The best reds are Rosso Cònero and Rosso Piceno.

Lazio

The two white wines of note here are Frascati and Est! Est!! Est!!! Frascati may be dry, medium or sweet. Est! Est!! Est!!! is either dry or has a hint of sweetness. Both wines are now more famous for their names than for the quality of the wine: The name Frascati flows and is easy to pronounce and remember. Est! Est!! Est!!! gets its name from the time when the Bavarian Bishop Fugger was preparing for a visit to Rome in 1111 AD. He sent his servant in advance to mark the doors of various inns that he would be passing en route with the word *'est'* ('it is') when the wine was good or *'non est'* when it was bad. When the servant came to Montefiascone, he was so impressed with the wine that he marked the door 'Est! Est!! Est!!!' The Bishop never did get to Rome but stayed happily at Montefiascone until he died.

Campania

From the slopes of Mount Vesuvius come the very well-known Lacryma Christi (tears of Christ) which may be red, white or rosé – the white is by far the best. Greco di Tufo and Fiano di Avellino are above average whites and the reds, Ravello and Taurasi, are becoming better known.

Sicily

This island is best known for its fortified dessert wine Marsala, a wine that is even more popular in the kitchen than at the table. It is used in Zabaglione as well as in veal and other dishes served *alla Marsala*. It became popular in Britain when Liverpudlian John Woodhouse began to develop the wine which he first exported from Marsala in 1773.

Marsala is made from two grapes, Insolia and Cattarato which together produce a dry white wine. *Vino cotto* (unfermented grape juice boiled in kettles to a syrup) is added, as is *vino passito*, a wine whose sweetness has been retained by the introduction of brandy during fermentation. The combination is put through a *solera* system (*see* Sherry, page 133) to blend and mature the wine. Today you will find Marsalas flavoured with all sorts of ingredients such as bananas, chocolate, coffee, almonds and even egg yolks – Marsala All'Uovo. Such additions are best avoided. The best-known shippers are Woodhouse & Co, Ingham Whittaker & Co and Florio & Co.

The best Sicilian table wines are Corvo (red and white) and Regaleali (red and white).

Sardinia

This island is especially noted for its sweet dessert wines such as Vernaccia di Sardegna, Moscato del Tempio, Malvasia di Sardegna and Anghelu Ruju. Of the table wines, the white Riviera del Corallo and the red Cannonau are best.

Veneto

The region is well known for its wine bar wines, like the dry white Soave and the popular reds, Valpolicella and Bardolino. Look out for the less well-known whites, Bianco di Custoza and Verduzzo, and the sparkling Prosecco.

Emilia-Romagna

This area is famous for Albana di Romagna, the first white wine in all of Italy to be been given the DOCG classification. Also well known are the red, white and rosé Lambrusco Frizzante (semi-sparkling wines).

Other wine regions

Basilicata is well known for its full-bodied red wine Aglianico del Vulture. In Lombardy (around Milan), Oltrepò Pavese makes red, white, rosé and sparkling wines. Friuli Venezia Giulia is well known for two red wines – Aquilea and Carso. Liguria is noted for Cinque Terra, dry or medium-sweet white wines. Abruzzi makes a good red wine Montepulciano d'Abruzzo. Molise also has a good red called Biferno. Puglia has two wines of note, the red Il Falcone and the pink Rosa del Golfo. Calabria is best known for Greco di Bianco, a lovely, big, creamy sweet wine (Vino Passito). Italy's smallest wine region Val d'Aosta, produces honest wines, almost always drunk locally.

Lebanon

Despite all the political troubles, red and white wines continue to be made in this war-torn land. The reds are much better than the whites, being made from a blend of Cabernet Sauvignon, Syrah and Cinsault grapes. Best examples are: Château Musar and Cuvée Musar which come from a single 140-hectare (345-acre) estate owned by the Hochar family. These wines have good ageing qualities.

Luxembourg

Luxembourg makes quite a number of thinish white wines from grapes such as Riesling, Elbling, Gewürztraminer and Sylvaner. There is also a slightly sparkling wine called Edelperl.

Malta

Cultivation of the vine is not easy in Malta where the climate can vary between torrential rain and scorching sunshine. The result is ordinary, even harsh wine. All types are made, with the Altar wine, the wine of the church, perhaps the best of all. There are pleasant dessert wines made from the Muscat grapes, and the winery Marsovin produces palatable red, white and rosé table wines. Others of note are Verdala Rosé, Lachryma Vitas (red and white), Coleiro (red and white) and the Farmers' Wine Co-operative which also produces red and white table wines.

Mexico

The home of Tequila is now getting a good reputation for wine. The best is made from varietal grapes: Cabernet Sauvignon, Barbera, Malbec, Merlot, Trebbiano, Grenache, and Zinfandel for red, and Chenin Blanc, Sauvignon Blanc, Riesling and Chardonnay for whites.

Well-known producers are:

Bodegas de Santo Tómas	Casa Madero
Casa Martell	Casa Pedro Domecq
Cavas de San Juan	Antonio Fernandez y Cia
Marqués de Aguayo	Vinicolo de Aguascalientes
	(the largest)

Morocco

When France established control of Morocco in 1912 much effort was made to upgrade the existing vineyards and to cultivate new ones. Most of the resulting wine was exported to France and the French colonies. Stricter French wine legislation now makes it impossible to import bulk Moroccan wine and sell it or export it under a French label, so the business is not what it was.

Plenty of red and white wines are made, with Fez and Meknes the chief wine-producing centres. Tarik and Chante Bled, full bodied and well balanced are typical examples. A unique wine of special interest is Gris de Boulaouane. It is a blush wine produced by the bleeding method. The grapes are suspended on sheets of white linen where they are self-pressed by their own weight. The juice slowly drips through the linen into containers and the resulting wine is aged in bottle, not in cask.

New Zealand

There has been a great improvement in New Zealand wines over the past ten years. Previously the country was associated with very ordinary fortified wines but today some excellent table wines are produced. The North Island, particularly Auckland and its surrounds, was the traditional homeland for the vine, but more significant vineyards are now to be found on the East Coast of the North Island in regions like Gisborne and Hawkes Bay and on the north edge of the South Island at Marlborough.

The first vines were planted in 1819 but the *Phylloxera* bug later took its toll. It was only in the 1970s and onwards that New Zealand came to grips with wine making. Many vineyards, previously planted with hybrid vines, were dug up and replanted with classic *Vitis vinifera* styles. Initially the Müller-Thurgau vine was the standard bearer, producing in abundance good dry and medium-dry wines. With its twin virtues of high yield and early ripening, the success of the Müller-Thurgau encouraged the planting of finer varietals such as Sauvignon Blanc, Chardonnay, Rhine Riesling, Gewürtztraminer, Sémillion, Pinot Blanc and Chenin Blanc. Although the Müller-Thurgau still accounts for about 30 per cent of the total output, it is the Sauvignon Blanc and the Chardonnay that are enhancing New Zealand's evergrowing reputation for fine white wine. Traditional and high-tech methods have, so far, failed to yield red wines of comparative quality, but experimentation with the Cabernet Sauvignon, Pinot Noir, Merlot and Pinotage vines continues.

The principal wineries in New Zealand are:

Babich	Cloudy Bay
Collard Brothers	Cooks
Coopers Creek	Delegat's Vineyard
Hunter's Wines	Mission Vineyards
Montana Wines	Nobilo's
Penfolds Wines	Selak Wines
Te Mata Estate	Villa Maria Estate

Portugal

For such a small country, Portugal produces a wonderful array of wines from table wines to the two classics, port and Madeira. The table wines, although not nearly as renowned as the fortified, reach a good average standard.

It was the Methuen Treaty of 1703 that brought Portuguese wine to the attention of the British wine drinkers. The terms of the Treaty between England and Portugal gave preferential treatment to the wines of Portugal over the traditional wine source suppliers, France and Germany. The wines then were extremely good value and have remained so to this day. A great variety of grapes are used in the production of these wines some of which are listed as follows:

Red wine grapes	White wine grapes
Agua Santa	Alvarinho
Alvarelhão	Arinto
Baga	Galego Dourado
Bastardo	Malvasia
Ramisco	Maria Gomes
Tinta Pinheira	Moscatel
Touriga	Rabigato

Wine regions

The main wine regions (excluding Madeira) are Bairrada, Beiras, Bucelas, Carcavelos, Colares, Dão, Estremadura, Minho, Setúbal, and Trás-os-Montes. These are considered below.

Bairrada

This region in the west of Portugal is known for good quality red wines which are rich in tannin when young but which, with patient ageing, become mellow and soft. White wine of average quality is made for local consumption as are some agreeable sparkling wines. The best of the latter comes from the Quinta do Ribeirinho and is made by the méthode traditionnelle.

Beiras

Situated in the far north of Portugal, this area produces some rosé wines around the town of Pinhel. The region is also noted for an excellent red wine Buçaco (Bussaco) and a good méthode traditionnelle sparkler called Raposeira. The white wines tend to be slightly acidic.

Bucelas

Located 26 km (16 miles) north of Lisbon, this small region produces white wines from the classic Arinto grape. However, despite the noble grape, the wines are very ordinary.

Carcavelos

This is a small vine-growing area between Lisbon and Estoril. It is especially noted for its fortified almond-flavoured wine which is made at the Quinta do Barão.

Colares

These vineyards are situated by the sea about 23 km (14 miles) north-west of Lisbon. Because of the nature of the soil, the *Phylloxera* aphid could not penetrate the great carpet of sand and consequently the vineyards escaped the terrible scourge. The Ramisco grape is used to great effect in the making of Colares, producing what many consider to be the premier red wine in Portugal. In youth the wine is very astringent but age matures and mellows it out to a silky smoothness. Some undistinguished white wine is also made.

Dão

Situated in the centre of Portugal, this area is famous for its full-bodied, strong, earthy red wines. They are mostly blended and have an agreeable smoothness because of their unusually rich glycerine content. The white Dão is greatly respected and appreciated locally, but not much reaches the export market.

Estremadura

This most prolific region in all Portugal is located 115 km (70 miles) north-west of Lisbon. The red and white wines are basic table wines meant for everyday drinking. Some of the whites can have a slight effervescence.

Minho

This region produces one of the most distinctive wines in Portugal. Vinho Verde (green wine) is made close to the Spanish border but it is not a green wine as such. The 'green' refers to the youth and personality of the wine (which comes from the use of some underripe grapes) and not the colour, which is either red or white. About three times more red than white is made, but curiously it is mainly the white variety that is exported.

The wines are made from grapes that are grown high up on pergolas. The grapes are picked early when they are slightly underripe. Because of this special method of vine cultivation the grapes get less reflected sunshine, resulting in proportionally less sugar but a higher malic acid content. Once bottled, the malic acid is broken down by naturally occurring bacteria. This evolution creates a malolactic fermentation which does not increase the alcohol content but produces a slight and agreeable effervescence. Vinho Verde should be drunk when it is young and vigorous. It does not require ageing.

Setúbal

Situated to the south-east of Lisbon, this area is famous for the fortified, intensely sweet, amber coloured Moscatel de Setúbal. The wine is usually aged in cask from 6 to 25 years, although younger and older examples are available. As it ages it develops an attractive honey flavour.

Trás-os-Montes

This region's name is synonymous with the internationally famous Mateus Rosé. The wine is so popular that the grape harvest of a great many vineyards in this rugged, mountainous region of the upper Douro River is given over to the production of the pink, pétillant wine. The wine is beautifully labelled and presented in flagon-shaped bottles which, however attractive, are difficult to store. The bottles, once prized as decorative lamp-shade bases, seem to have lost their appeal in this respect.

Label language

Adega	winery
Colheita	vintage
Engarrafado	bottled by
Garrafeira	tells you the wine has matured in cask and bottle for some time – at least one year for white wine and two years for red wine
Quinta	estate
Região Demarcada	the wine comes from a legally demarcated region

Reserva	a quality aged wine
Selo de Origem	seal of origin
Denominacao de Origem	guarantee of origin and quality, similar to DOC in Italy
Vinho espumante	a sparkling wine
Vinho generoso	a strong, dessert wine

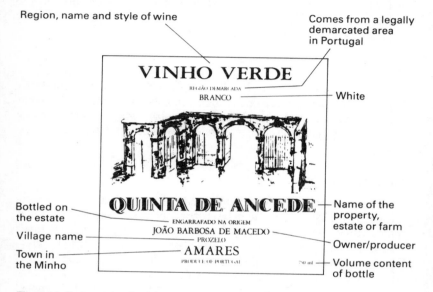

Region, name and style of wine — Comes from a legally demarcated area in Portugal

VINHO VERDE
REGIÃO DEMARCADA
BRANCO — White

QUINTA DE ANCEDE — Name of the property, estate or farm
ENGARRAFADO NA ORIGEM
JOÃO BARBOSA DE MACEDO — Owner/producer
PROZELO
AMARES
PRODUCE OF PORTUGAL   750 ml — Volume content of bottle

Bottled on the estate — Village name — Town in the Minho

Fig. 5.14 Portuguese wine label

Port

This great after dinner drink is made from a combination of grapes grown in the upper Douro Valley, in northern Portugal. At a precise moment during fermentation the wine is transferred to vats where sufficient local high-strength brandy (aguardente) is added to halt the fermentation. This not only fortifies the wine but ensures the retention of some of the grape sugar, giving a finished product that is soft, sweet and smooth.

Port is a blended product of wines from different *quintas* (farms or estates) and, although made in the Douro, the wine is matured in *lodges* (cellars) in Vila Nova de Gaia across the river from Oporto.

There are two main styles of port, each with its own subcategories:

Wood port

This is port that has spent all its life maturing in cask and is ready for drinking once bottled. Examples are white, ruby and tawny port.

White port
Made from white grapes, it is usually sweet but sometimes an apéritif style is produced. An example of the latter is Cockburn's Dry Tang which is deliciously refreshing either chilled or with ice and a slice of lemon.

Ruby port
This type of port is kept in cask for about five years until it becomes ruby in colour. It is a basic port often drunk with lemonade and other mixtures.

Tawny port
Tawny port is kept in cask for up to ten years (more for an aged tawny) or until it fades to a tawny colour. Although, like ruby, it is a blend of different years, it can be a mellow, real quality wine.

Bottle port

This is port that has matured mainly, or at least some time, in bottle. Examples include crusted, late-bottled vintage (LBV), vintage character and vintage.

Crusted port
This is a blend of vintage quality ports kept in cask for up to four years. When bottled it throws sediment or crust as it matures – hence the name.

Late-Bottled Vintage (LBV)
LBV is a vintage-style port, matured in wood for about six years, and then bottled where it will continue to improve.

Vintage character port
This port is a blended good quality wine of different years. Rather similar in style to LBV but not as classy, it is wooded for about four years and is ready to drink soon after being bottled.

Vintage port
Vintage port is made from grapes grown in an outstanding year,

producing the finest port available. Matured in wood for 2, sometimes 3 years, it is kept in bottles for up to 20 years or more so that it matures slowly. It is always binned and handled with the whitewash splash or label uppermost so as not to disturb the sediment.

Like crusted port, the vintage variety should always be decanted (*see* page 27). When dining, the decanter is traditionally passed to the person to one's left (the way of the sun or, more romantically, so it is given from the heart).

Brand names

The following brand names are generally associated with port:

Cockburn's	Ferreira	Quinta do Noval
Croft	Fonseca	Sandeman
Delaforce	Graham's	Taylor's
Dow's	Gonzales Byass	Warre's

Madeira

When the island was first discovered in 1418 it was covered with trees and was given the name Madeira (meaning 'wood'). Legend has it that it took seven years to burn the trees to ashes. The ash enriched the soil, providing a suitable home for the vine and sugar cane. The wine Madeira was first fortified in the eighteenth century to strengthen it for long sea voyages. Casks of wine were used as ballast as ships journeyed from Funchal (the capital) to the Portuguese colonies in South America and the Far East.

It was soon discovered that the combination of heat and agitation as the wine was carried to and from the tropics improved the taste of the wine. Later the *estufa* system was introduced to give similar results. The estufa (stove or heated room) has concrete vats in which the wine is gradually heated to an agreed temperature limit, usually not more than 50°C (120°F) and then slowly brought back to normal temperature. This 'cooking' of the wine, which can take four to five months, imparts colour and a special flavour unique to Madeira. The wine is blended and matured by the solera system (*see* page 133).

Styles of Madeira

There are four main styles of Madeira, each of which is named after the principal grape used:

Sercial
This is the driest Madeira produced. It makes a good apéritif chilled or with ice.

Verdelho
A sweeter richer wine that is also used in the kitchen to flavour soups and sauces.

Bual
Pronounced 'boal', this is a full, deep golden wine that is sweet without being cloying on the palate.

Malmsey
A luscious dessert wine that is darkish brown in colour. It is initially very sweet on the palate but, like all Madeiras, it leaves you with a 'dry goodbye' which is a quite delicious contrast.

Brand names

The following are the brand names frequently associated with Madeira wine:

Blandy Brothers	Leacock	Rutherford & Miles
Cossart Gordon	Lomelino	

Romania

Romanian wines have made little impact on world markets even though they are very reasonably priced. Those to look out for are the late-harvested Gewürztraminer and the Rosé Edelbeerenlese made from botrytized grapes (grapes attacked by *Botrytis cinerea*). The light red Valea Lunga, the spicy red Nicoresti, the fulsome Tohani and Valea Calugareasca (Valley of the Monks) are all good with food. Last but not least is Cotnari, the lush white dessert wine made after the style of Tokay.

—————————— **South Africa** ——————————

The first vines were planted in South Africa in 1654, but it was not until the nineteenth century that their wines became popular worldwide. In recent years political pressure has curtailed the sale of South African wines internationally, but with political changes the situation is improving for South African wines and their good to fine wines are now being sold on merit, like all other wines are. Most bottles show a coloured seal of origin known locally as the 'bus ticket': blue guarantees the location of production; red guarantees that at least 75 per cent of the wine was made in the year indicated on the label; green certifies that at least 75 per cent of the wine was made from the indicated grape; and gold suggests a wine of superior quality.

In 1918 the Ko-öperatiewe Wijnbouwers Vereniging (KWV) – the Co-operative Winegrowers Association – was formed to organise and supervise the production methods and marketing of the industry. They have done a good job and about 90 per cent of the wine exported comes from members of this association. Incidentally, the KWV cellars at Paarl cover 10 hectares (25 acres) and are capable of holding 113.5 million litres (30 million gallons) of wine.

White wine

The best white wines come from the areas around Stellenbosch, Paarl and Tulbagh, with Riesling, Sauvignon Blanc, Clairette Blanche and Steen the favoured grapes. Owing to the hot climate the wines undergo a slow, temperature-controlled fermentation to preserve quality. South African white wines are meant to be drunk young when they are lively and refreshing. Good examples are:

Fleur du Cap Sauvignon Blanc   Twee Jongegezellen
KWV Chenin Blanc   Theuniskraal Riesling
Groot Constantia Gewürztraminer   Zonnebloem Noble Late
                                                 Harvest Superior

Red wine

The reds are mainly produced in Constantia, Durbanville, Paarl and Stellenbosch, where Cabernet Sauvignon, Shiraz, Gamay, Pinot Noir and Pinotage (Pinot Noir and Cinsault) are the most used grapes. South African reds may be light- or full-bodied. Look out for:

Zonnebloem Cabernet Sauvignon KWV Roodeberg
Culemborg Pinotage Château Libertas
Nederburg Cabernet Backsberg Estate

Other drinks

South Africa makes the best sherry outside Spain, particularly the fino variety which is really outstanding. Flor, a thin layer of yeast fungus forms naturally on these wines, which enhances the flavour as they mature in cask. The best finos come from Stellenbosch and Paarl and are matured by the solera system. The sweeter sherries are made in Worcester, Robertson, Montagu and Bonnievale, areas which also produce dessert wines such as the Muscatels and many styles of port.

The Oude Meester Company make a fine brandy called Oude Meester (Old Master) and the best-known liqueur from South Africa is the tangerine flavoured Van der Hum, meaning 'What's its name?'.

Spain

Spain has the largest area of vineyards in the world yet it is only the world's third largest producer. Closer planting of vines and improved methods of viticulture will, eventually, improve volume, but quality is already there as the country produces excellent wine in a wide variety of styles. The production is controlled by 28 denominations of origin – Denominación de Origen (DO) – which regulate viticulture and vinification standards and set guidelines for marketing, promotions and sales. Denominación de Origen Calificada is a new super category established in 1991 to acknowledge fine quality wines. Of all the wines produced sherry is the most famous.

Fig. 5.15 Wine-producing regions of Spain

Sherry

This fortified wine is produced in southern Spain in the Provence of Cadiz. The vineyards are situated around three towns, Jerez de la Frontera, Sanlúcar de Barrameda and Puerto de Santa Maria. While some of the vines are grown in clay (*barros*) and sand (*arenas*) the most hospitable soil for the two grapes used – Listan (Palomino) and Pedro Ximénez (PX)– is chalk (*albariza*). About 85 per cent of the vineyards are under the Palomino vine which produces a basic dry

Fig. 5.16 Flor on surface of wine

white wine, while the PX grapes are used to enrich, with sweetness, the heavier styles of sherry destined for export. As all sherries are naturally dry, any sweetness has to be added.

In winter the new wine is put into small nursery casks or *criaderas* (cradles) to see how it is going to develop. It is carefully monitored and in spring a yeast-like fungus (*Saccharomyces beticus)*, also known as flor (flower), will develop on the surface of some of the wines. This spontaneous occurrence is an indication that the wine will develop into the highly-prized, light, delicate wine known as *fino*. Absence of flor shows the wine is destined to become a full-bodied *oloroso*. Of course there are variations of these two major classifications.

Fig. 5.17 Solera blending system

The finos are now fortified up to 15.5 per cent volume of alcohol by the addition of local high-strength brandy; the olorosos are topped up to 18 per cent by volume. Both types usually get a second fortification before sale – bottled sherries have an alcoholic strength of between 16 and 21 per cent by volume. The sweeter styles are more heavily fortified.

Before bottling, all sherries must go through the unique maturing and blending system of the solera. The solera is a series of casks placed one on top of the other five or six scales high. When wine is required for sale it is drawn from the bottom scale of casks – only one-third is allowed to be drawn off each year. The void is replenished by wine from the scale immediately above. This continues upwards, with the more mature wines being continually refreshed by younger wines – the youngest of all being in the top scale. Finally, the wine for sale is blended and adjusted, if necessary, for colour, sweetness and alcohol content. The skill of the blender (the sauce chef of the wine trade) ensures consistency of the product.

Some old unblended sherries known as Almacenista are also made. These dry, exceptional wines are of supreme distinction and are used primarily as blenders to give character and uplift to the more mundane styles. However, some firms are now selling them as a special brand in their own right.

Styles of sherry

Fino
A fragrant, delicate, pale and extremely dry sherry. It has a powerful bouquet and pleasing flavour.

Manzanilla
A style of fino made from grapes grown by the sea at Sanlúcar de Barrameda and matured in local *bodegas* (cellars). Proximity to the ocean breeze and the unique thickness of the flor imparts a salty and attractive bitter tang to this wine.

Amontillado
Slightly fuller and deeper in colour than fino, it is a member of the fino family and has a pronounced nutty flavour. This wine gets its name from its similarity in style to Montilla wine produced near Cordoba 190 km (120 miles) away.

Palo Cortado
Somewhere in style between an amontillado and an oloroso. It is very popular in Spain and difficult to find elsewhere.

Oloroso
Rich and deep coloured with a generous, full flavour, it is sweetened by Pedro Ximénez grape concentrate known as *dulce*. The name oloroso encompasses all the cream, brown and East India sherries on the market. However, many of the pale cream sherries marketed are not true olorosos but are sweetened finos.

Service

Fino, manzanilla and amontillado sherries are best served chilled or on the rocks. Other styles may be served straight from the bottle, ideally into a copita – the traditional sherry glass. Sixteen measures can be obtained from a normal (75 cl) bottle.

Sherry shippers

The best-known sherry shippers (producers) are:

Gonzales Byas	Garvey	Harveys	Sandeman
Pedro Domecq	Williams & Humbert	La Riva	
Croft	Duff Gordon	Osborne	

Table wines

Nearly all the best wines of Spain come under the Denominación de Origen (DO) laws, which are similar to the AOC of France and DOC of Italy. Whereas sherry is produced in the south, most of the finer table wines are produced in the north in regions such as Rioja and Catalonia.

Rioja

Tempranillo, Garnacha, Graciano and Mazuelo grapes produce Spain's famous red wines. The Rio Oja, a tributory of the Ebro, gives its name to the locality which is divided into three regions: Rioja Alta (the best Rioja area), Alavesa (the next best) and Rioja Baja. The wines are big, soft, rich and mellow with a distinctive oaky flavour derived from being matured in small 225-litre oak casks for up to six years. Best examples are Marqués de Murrieta, Marqués de Riscal, Marqués de Cáceres, Vina Tondonia, La Rioja Alta, of which the style Viña Ardanza Reserva 904 is quite outstanding, and CVNE (Compania Vinicola del Norte de Espana).

Some good white Riojas from Malvasia and Viura grapes are also made, such as Marqués de Cáceres, Marqués de Murrieta, Viña Soledad and CVNE.

Catalonia

Penedès
Excellent sparkling and still white and red wines are made here. The sparkling variety is sold under the generic name of *cava* (cellar). Made by the metodo tradicional, it is widely available under propri-etory brand names such as Gran Codorníu, Freixenet Cordon Negro, Segura Viudas and Castellblanch Brut Zero.

The white wines of Penedès are a revelation especially Torres Gran Viña Sol Green Label made from Parellada and Sauvignon Blanc grapes. Torres also makes Viña Esmeralda, a medium-sweet wine made from Muscat and Gewürztraminer grapes. The dry, crisp Jean León Chardonnay and Marqués de Allela are produced near the suburbs of Barcelona. Of the red wines, Torres again produces the pedigree wines Gran Coronas (Cabernet Sauvignon and Tempranillo) and Grand Coronas Black Label (Cabernet Sauvignon and Cabernet Franc) – the latter is a really wonderful wine. Jean León's Cabernet Sauvignon is also excellent.

Ribera del Duero
Ribera del Duero produces, in small quantities, the great classic red, Vega Sicilia Unico Reserva – a wine that ages well up to 30 years and is considered one of the finest reds in the world. It is made from the Cabernet Sauvignon, Malbec and Merlot grapes and is frightfully expensive. Tinto Valbuena is another fine, slightly less expensive, wine produced in the same bodega near Valladolid. Look out for Bodega Alejandro Fernandez Tinta Pesquera and Bodega Hermanos Perez Viña Pedrosa which offer much better value.

Other wine-producing regions

Navarra
The region of Navarra is located on the border of Rioja and spills over into Rioja Baja. The red, white and rosé wines get heavy media promotion as alternatives to Rioja, but they are far too robust by comparison. Watch for the names Bodegas Villafranca Monte Ory Reserva, Julián Chivite Gran Feudo Tinto, Agro Navarra Camponuevo Tinto, Señorío de Sarría Viña Ecoyen Tinto and Viña del Perdon Tinto.

Andalucia
This region produces a lovely fortified dessert wine, Málaga, once known as 'Mountain', that is rarely seen nowadays outside Spain. Made from the Pedro Ximénez and Muscat grapes, it undergoes the blending and maturing process of the solera. The best style is Lágrima ('tear' – as in 'weep') made from grapes which are self-pressed by their own weight. Bodegas Barcelo and Scholtz Hermanos make quality Málaga.

La Mancha
The Midi of Spain produces a vast wine lake of table wines – often the

base for Sangria and headaches! Valdepeñas (Valley of Stones) produces
sound red and white wines which are used in and around Madrid.

Alicante
This region is best known for its rosé and for the extremely dark red
Vino de Doble Pasta – made by adding a double quantity of grape
skins which deeply darkens the colour during fermentation.

Ampurdán (Costa Brava)
This area is best known for its sparkling wine, Perelada, which is
made by the metodo tradicional.

Label language

Abocado	medium sweet
Año	year
Blanco	white
Bodega	winery
Cava	cellar or generic name for sparkling wine made by the metodo tradicional
Clarete	light red table wine
Cosecha	vintage
Denominación de Origen (DO)	a quality guarantee, ensures geographical origin
Consejo Regulado	the regulating body. Its stamp on the label ensures authenticity
Embotellado por	bottled by
Espumoso	sparkling
Gran Reserva	the highest grade for a quality wine which has spent two years in cask and three years in bottle
Reserva	the next best grade – the wine has matured one year in case and two years in bottle
Rosado	rosé, pink
Seco	dry
Semi-seco	medium dry
Sin crianza	without wood age
Tinto	red
Vendimia	vintage harvest
Viña	vineyard
Vino de mesa	table wine

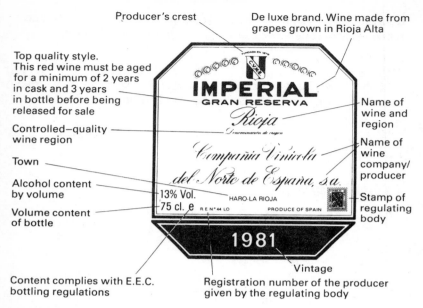

Producer's crest

De luxe brand. Wine made from grapes grown in Rioja Alta

Top quality style. This red wine must be aged for a minimum of 2 years in cask and 3 years in bottle before being released for sale

Controlled–quality wine region

Town

Alcohol content by volume

Volume content of bottle

Name of wine and region

Name of wine company/ producer

Stamp of regulating body

IMPERIAL
GRAN RESERVA
Rioja
Denominación de origen

*Compañia Viníola
del Norte de España, s.a.*

13% Vol.   HARO·LA RIOJA
·75 cl. e   R.E. Nº 44 LO   PRODUCE OF SPAIN

1981

Content complies with E.E.C. bottling regulations

Registration number of the producer given by the regulating body

Vintage

Fig. 5.18 Spanish wine label

Switzerland

Without a doubt, the quality of Swiss wine is consistently good but the wines are expensive to buy and fairly difficult to obtain. The country is made up of 25 *cantons* (districts), most of which produce wine, with the French-speaking cantons producing the best of all.

Valais

The Valais wine-growing area extends along the entire valley of the Rhône from Viège to Martigny. The region produces good red and white wines – the red Dôle is well considered. Made from Gamay and Pinot Noir grapes, it has an affinity to the fulsome Burgundy reds. Petite Dôle is also an interesting red wine made solely from Pinot Noir grapes. Of the whites, Fendant made from the Chasselas grapes is best, but there are other good styles such as the Johannisberg. Vin du Glacier is a white wine made in the Anniviers Valley and then taken to caves in the mountains near the glaciers to mature in larchwood casks for up to 15 years. Malvoisie is an estate-bottled, straw-coloured, dessert wine made from late-gathered noble rot grapes.

The Vaud

Vaud vineyards are located along the shores of Lake Geneva (Lac Léman) and include three smaller districts: La Côte, Lavaux and Chablais. The area is generally known for its fine white wines made from the Chasselas (Dorin locally) grape. Prime examples are Dézaley, Mont-sur-Rolle, Saint Saphorin and Aigle Clos de Murailles. The latter is one of the finest and most expensive of all Swiss wines.

Neuchâtel

Neuchâtel produces light fragrant white wines mostly from the Chasselas grape. Some are pétillant and produce the famous Neuchâtel stars when poured from a height into the glass. There is also a red Pinot Noir wine called Cortaillod and a pink one called Oeil de Perdrix (partridge eye) made from the same grape.

Turkey

Much of the grape production in Turkey is used for table grapes and sultanas, but some reasonable wine is also made. The majority of the wine is red, good examples being Villa Doluca, Hosbag, Buzbag and Trakya Kirmisi. The dry Trakya made from the Sémillon grape is the best of the whites.

The former Soviet Union (CIS)

With modern technology and expertise and greater awareness of the international market requirements, these wines are bound to improve. At the moment, they are on the sticky, sweet side, which suits the Russian palate well. Moldova, on the Romanian border, pro-duces Negru de Purkar, a high-strength red wine with good ageing potential. It is made from the Cabernet Sauvignon, Saperavi and Rara Neagra grapes. Fetjaska is the principal grape for white wines.

Massandra in the Crimea is the dessert wine centre using mainly the Muscatel grape. Good sparkling wines such as Kaffia and Krim are made by the méthode traditionnelle. Georgia, with its vineyards in the valley of the River Rion, makes decent red wines like Mukuzani and Saperavi and straw-coloured whites Tsinandal and Rkatiseli. Some sparkling wine is made and marketed as Champanski. Russia produces mainly white and sparkling wine from around Krosnador. Stavropol, east of Krosnador, makes dryish white as well as the good dessert wine Muscatel Praskoveiski. In Armenia, Port and Sherry-style wines are made as well as table wines like the red Norashen, the white Echmiadzin and the pink Pamid. Perla (white) and Iskra (red) are the sparklers.

—— United States of America ——

Although there were wine-growing grapes found in North America from as early as 1562, the modern wine industry dates from 1933 when Prohibition ended. Known also as The Volstead Act, Prohibition (1919–33) was America's stab at trying to forbid the distribution and sale of all alcoholic beverages. It came about as a direct reaction to the drinking of hard liquor which, it was feared, would lead to alcohol abuse and threaten the quality of family life. The effect on the wine industry was disastrous and during those 14 'dry' years most of the vineyards lay fallow. Some survived by growing grapes for home wine makers or by making sacramental wine for churches or by making tonic wine which was intended for medical use.

After Prohibition, wine stocks were depleted and many wine growers, old and new, either through greed or a lack of ethics, planted high-yielding vines which inevitably led to a profusion of low-quality wines. The industry's reputation plummeted – cheap port, sherry and Madeira-style wines abounded and sweetness did indeed cover a multitude of sins. Some appalling blends of table wines were also sold under generic names such as chablis, chianti and claret without having even a passing resemblance to the originals. But slowly things began to improve. The Wine Institute, based in California, was established to help and encourage the growers to make better wine and to educate the general public about wine and its uses. The Department of Viticulture and Oenology set up by the University of California at

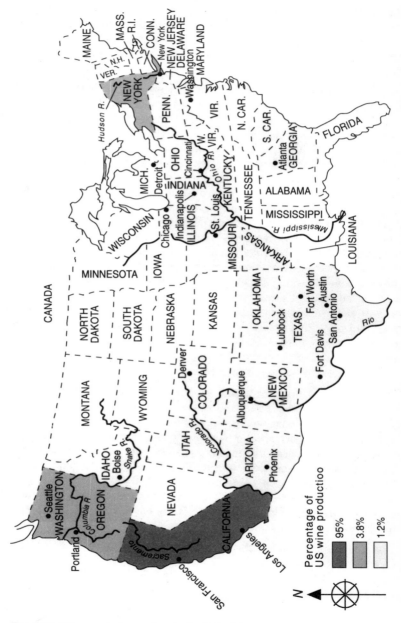

Fig. 5.19 Wine-producing regions in the United States

Davis conducted extensive research into all aspects of viticulture and vinification. The combined strategy was to ensure that the right vines were planted in the right soil and in the right growing environment and that science and technology could be used to give nature a helping hand.

As a result of these initiatives the quality of wine got better and better, and with more and more Americans travelling abroad and discovering the delights of food and wine as a partnership, there was an increased interest in the art of good living. People started to abandon hard liquor and beer in favour of wine, and to drink varietal wine (wine named after a principal grape) rather than generic or fortified wines. The wine boom came in the mid 1960s and 1970s. It was focused mainly on California where the number of wineries doubled within a decade. The momentum spread from California to the Pacific North-West, across to the Midwest Plains and onward to the Atlantic North-East. By 1985 there were 1,300 commercial wineries in North America. Many of them were small and family-owned, others were started by people disillusioned with their previous professions and lured into wine making either by a romantic notion or by a pioneering sense of adventure. Their successes encouraged others to follow, but all was not well. Traditionally American wine was made for home consumption, but it was noticed in the 1970s that while production and sales were increasing, the number of American wine drinkers were not. The home market became saturated so attention turned towards the highly competitive international market.

The big breakthrough came on 24 May 1976 at a blind-tasting in Paris, where the finest palates in the land judged that the Californian Chardonnay and Cabernet Sauvignon wines were as good as, if not better than, the best similar varietal wines that France could produce. After the shock and media hype the wine gates opened and American wines, because of their quality and style, were appreciated internationally by a wine-discerning public. In 1984 more than 3 million cases were exported. In 1992 the export figure reached 18 million plus cases with the United Kingdom, Canada and Japan taking the major share.

It is estimated that 43 of the 50 states cultivate the vine for making wine. Of these, California is the prime region producing 95 per cent of the crop, New York State 2 per cent and Washington State and its neighbour Oregon 1.8 per cent. The other states' output totals

1.2 per cent. The Bureau of Alcohol, Tobacco and Firearms (BATF) is the controlling body for the drinks industry. In 1978 it conceived a form of appelation known as Approved Viticultural Areas (AVAs). Briefly they stipulate that:

- Varietal wines must use a minimum of 75 per cent of the grape named on the label;
- When a geographic source is indicated, at least 75 per cent of the wine must come from there;
- Wines from a specific vintage or from a nominated particular estate, must have at least 95 per cent of that wine in the bottle.

It must be said that not all wineries adhere to these constrictions. They blend in whatever proportions suit their needs. Basically there are two qualities of wine made in the United States.

Table wine

These popular table wines are reliable, attractive, inexpensive and made in huge quantities by the ultra-modern, fully automated wineries. Technically sound, the wines are blended to a recipe. We would call them carafe wines. In America they are known as 'jug wines' as they are traditionally sold by the jugful in diners and restaurants throughout the country.

Premium wines

The best quality is known as premium wine, made by proprietors working on a smaller scale. These designer wines are crafted to the highest standard in boutique wineries especially in California. A few of the owners are hippy wine makers – having had a previous professional occupation before dropping out and opting for wine making. Most, however, are graduates of the Wine College of the University of California at Davis. These masters of cultured yeast use meticulous control of fermentation temperatures and technical innovations to help nature in making good wines great. They are now producing wines of real quality, concentrating on elegance and subtlety rather than on alcohol and powerfully dominating flavours. Some of the sparkling wines being made are also outstanding. It is just a pity that some producers persist in calling the bubbly product – which can be made by the traditional method, closed tank method or the transfer method – Champagne, which it is not.

The most important wine-producing regions in the United States are California, New York State, Washington State, Oregon, Texas and Maryland.

California

Spanish missionaries first brought the vine to California towards the end of the eighteenth century. By 1831 Jean Louis Vignes, a Frenchman from Bordeaux, was producing good wine and distilling good quality brandy. With the arrival of Agoston Haraszthy, a Hungarian political exile, in 1849 a real wine industry began to develop. By 1857 Haraszthy had established his own, now famous Buena Vista vineyard in Sonoma County. In 1861 he was sent to Europe by the Governor of California charged with bringing back the widest selection of European vines. He returned with over 100,000 cuttings of 1,400 varieties. By 1875, California was producing 18 million litres (4 million gallons) of wine annually, based on the classical *Vitis vinifera* stock.

With its benign climate, accommodating soil and ideal aspects, California is a natural home for the vine. Many of the vineyard sites are also blessed by a unique microclimate. The Californian coastal fog shrouds the vines throughout the summer from the fierce morning sun rays. This benefits the quality of the grapes by slowing down and prolonging the ripening process. The main grapes used are the European varieties Cabernet Sauvignon, Pinot Noir and Merlot as well as the indigenous Zinfandel for red wines. The Chardonnay, Sauvignon Blanc (Fumé Blanc) and Johannisberg Riesling are the principal white grapes in use.

The major areas of production are the classic Napa Valley and the Sonoma Valley, Mendocino and the central coast from Monterey to Santa Barbara. Some of the best producers are listed by their speciality grape variety below.

Red wines

Zinfandel	Ridge Vineyards, Buena Vista, Joseph Phelps, Ch. Montelena, Ravenswood, Preston, Beringer, Stevenot, Storybook, Fetzer, Boeger

Fig. 5.20 Californian wine producing areas

Cabernet Sauvignon   Robert Mondavi, Trefethen, Jordan, Joseph Phelps, Heitz Cellar (Martha's Vineyard and Bella Oaks Especially), Freemark Abbey, Stags Leap, Ridge Vineyards, Mayacamas, Jekel, Iron Horse, Clos du Val, Buena Vista, Almedén, Beaulieu, Simi, The Christian Brothers, Rubicon and Paul Masson.

Pinot Noir	Chalone, Acacia, Trefethen, Robert Mondavi (the Reserve wines especially), Kalin, Saintsbury, Sanford, Wild Horse, Almadén, Hanzell
Merlot	Clos du Bois, Firestone Vineyard, Stags Leap, Sterling Vineyards, Clos du Val, Rutherford Hill, Inglenook, Jordan, Boeger.

White wines

Chardonnay	Robert Mondavi, Trefethen, Stags Leap, Acacia, Ch. St Jean, Mark West, Monticello, Freemark Abbey, Ch. Montelena, Mayacamas, Chalone, Edna Valley, Firestone Vineyard, Alexander Valley, Buena Vista, Simi, Wente, Mantanzas Creek
Sauvignon Blanc (Fumé Blanc)	Dry Creek, Robert Mondavi, Sterling Vineyards, Mantanzas Creek, Beringer, Gallo, Callaway, Concannon Vineyard
Johannisberg Riesling	Château St Jean, Joseph Phelps, Jekel, Firestone Vineyard, Boeger
Sparkling wines – méthode traditionnelle	Schramsberg, Domaine Chandon, Piper Sonoma, Iron Horse, Ch. St Jean, Mumm Cuvée Napa, Jordan 'J', Korbel, Roederer Estate

---

THE RETURN OF PHYLLOXERA

Tragically the vine louse has re-emerged and is destroying a substantial number of Californian vineyards. Rootstock previously thought to be immune to the aphid has been found wanting and has succumbed to this new strain of Phylloxera known as Biotype B. A huge replanting programme is in progress using aphid-resistant rootstock.

New York State

Traditionally, the New York wine industry was based on the use of *Vitis labrusca* vines (Concord, Catawba, Delaware, Dutchess, Ives and

Niagara). Although these produced reasonable fortified and sparkling wines, their table wine had a distinctive musky aroma and flavour – generally described as 'foxy'. The flavour is so exotic it is not really appreciated outside New York. The *labrusca* vines were chosen initially to withstand the arctic conditions of winter. Later it was discovered that other species can also cope with the extremes of climate. Recently hybrids based on *labrusca* and *vinifera* vines (Vidal Blanc, Seyval Blanc, Chelois, Baco Noir, De Chaunac, Aurore, Maréchal Foch) were developed to temper the notorious taste. Even more recently the classic *vinifera* vines have also been successfully planted as anybody who has tasted Wagner's Chardonnay will confirm.

The main areas of production are Finger Lakes, Long Island and the Hudson River Valley.

Finger Lakes

Here *Vitis labrusca* hybrids and *Vitis vinifera* vines are grown to produce grapes for wine. The current trend is to use the classic *vinifera* vines with the whites – Chardonnay, Riesling and Gewürztraminer – proving particularly successful.

Best-known producers are:

Canandaigua Wine Company	Vinifera Vineyards
Glenora Wine Cellars	Wagner Vineyards
Knapp Vineyards	Wiemer Vineyard

Splendid sparkling wine, made by the classical method, is a feature of the region. Prime brands are Gold Seal, Great Western and Taylor.

Long Island

Wineries in Long Island are concentrating more and more on Vitis vinifera vines and are now successfully cultivating Merlot, Cabernet Sauvignon and Cabernet Franc for red wines, and Chardonnay and Sauvignon Blanc for whites. Most of the wineries are situated in the North Fork Peninsula. The best-known producers are:

Bedell Cellars	Lenz Vineyards
Bridgehampton Winery	Palmer Vineyards
Hargrave Vineyards	Pindar Vineyards

Hudson River Valley

This is the oldest wine region in New York State. Here the hybrid Seyval Blanc reigns supreme, but the current vogue is for *vinifera* vines – Cabernet Sauvignon and Pinot Noir for red wines and Chardonnay and Riesling for white wines. Benmarl Wine Company, Clinton Vineyards, Millbrook Vineyards and the Rivendell Winery have all established good reputations.

Oregon

Oregon's vineyards are concentrated in the Willamette Valley, Umpqua Valley and Rogue Valley. Although the general climatic conditions are cool, the coast range in the west and the Cascade mountains in the east prevents them from being extreme. Mostly *Vitis vinifera* vines are cultivated: Chardonnay, Müller-Thurgau, Sauvignon Blanc and Pinot Gris for white wines, and Pinot Noir, Merlot and Cabernet Sauvignon for reds.

The best producers are:

Sokol Blosser	Tualatin Vineyards
Eyrie Vineyards	Elk Cove
Peter F. Adams	Arterberry Winery (noted for its sparkling wine)
Amity Vineyards	Adelsheim Vineyards
Knudsen-Erath	Domaine Drouhin
Ponzi	Willamette Valley Vineyards

Washington State

Washington vineyards are *Phylloxera*-free and so the vines in cultivation are ungrafted. With a hot, arid climate, irrigation is necessary. The sweltering summer days are counterbalanced by cool temperatures at night so the grapes have a healthy acidity. Vitis vinifera vines were first introduced in the 1950s. Chardonnay, Sauvignon Blanc, Sémillon for white wine, and Cabernet Sauvignon and Merlot for reds are all cultivated successfully. The main vineyards are grouped in Yakima Valley, Columbia Valley, Walla Walla Valley and Spokane. Château Ste Michelle, Associated Vintners, Hinzerling, Preston Wine Cellars, the Hogue Cellars and Leonetti Cellar are the best-known producers.

Texas

With its extreme, arid, climate it is hard to imagine Texas as being vine friendly. Yet, due to modern, sophisticated irrigation which uses the drip method to water each vine individually, the grape has been successfully cultivated. Texas produces over 1 million cases of wine annually and is now the fourth largest wine-producing state in the United States. The three major areas of production are the High Plains near Lubbock, Austin in the Hill Country and West Texas. Mostly *vinifera* vines are cultivated – Sauvignon Blanc, Chenin Blanc and Chardonnay for whites and Pinot Noir and Zinfandel for reds.

The labels to look out for are:

Fall Creek Vineyards
La Buena Vida Vineyards
Llano Estacado Winery
Messino Hof Wine Cellars
Cap Rock Winery

Pheasant Ridge Winery
Ste Genevieve Vineyards
Texas Vineyards
Val Verde Winery

Maryland

Phillip Wagner, publisher of *The Baltimore Sun*, was the pioneering spirit behind Maryland wines. Having previously dabbled in home wine making he established, in 1945, the Boordy vineyards and introduced the French/American hybrid Seyval Blanc vine and others to the Atlantic north-east. He also successfully experimented with *Vitis vinifera* vines such as Chardonnay and Riesling and the red Cabernet Sauvignon before his retirement in 1980. Boordy is still the biggest vineyard in Maryland, producing in excess of 8,000 cases yearly. Other good producers are Byrd Vineyards, Berrywine Plantations, Basignani Winery, Elk Run Vineyards, Fiore Winery, Loew Vineyards, Montbray Wine Cellars, Woodhall Vineyards and Ziem Vineyards. So, from a casual cottage industry Maryland wineries have grown commercially and in importance. They now produce, for sale, well over 600,000 bottles annually. Look out for labels showing Chardonnay for white wines and Cabernet Sauvignon for red wines.

Notable wine producers in other States

Massachusetts	Chicama Vineyards, Commonwealth Winery
Rhode Island	Diamond Hill Vineyards, Prudence Island Vineyards, Sakonnet Vineyards
Connecticut	Chamard Vineyards, Clarke Vineyard, Crosswoods Vineyards, Di Grazia Vineyards, Haight Vineyard, Hamlet Hill Vineyard, Hopkins Vineyard
Pennsylvania	Alegro Vineyards, Chaddsford Winery
New Jersey	Alba Vineyard, Four Sisters Winery, Gross' Highland Winery, Kings Road Vineyard, Renault Winery, Tewksbury Wine Cellars, Tomasello Winery
Virginia	Barboursville Winery, Ingleside Plantation Vineyards, Meredyth Vineyards, Montdomaine Cellars, Oakencroft Vineyard, Piedmont Vineyards, Prince Michel Vineyard, Rapidan River Vineyards
North Carolina	Château Baltimore
Florida	Lafayette Vineyards
Tennessee	Laurel Hill Vineyard, Tennessee Valley Winery
Georgia	Château Elan
Ohio	Breitenbach Wine Cellars, Chalet Debonne Vineyards, Firelands Wine Company, Grand River Wine Company, Markko Vineyard, Meier's Wine Cellars
Michigan	Boskydel Vineyard, Fenn Valley Vineyards, Grand Traverse Vineyards, St Julian Wine Company
Indiana	The Bloomington Winery, Château Thomas Winery, Easley Winery, Huber Orchard Winery, Oliver Wine Company, Possum Trot Vineyards, St Wendel Cellars, Villa Milan Vineyard
Minnesota	Alexis Bailly Vineyard
Wisconsin	Wollersheim Winery
Missouri	Carver Wine Cellars, Hermannhof Winery, Montelle Vineyards, Mount Pleasant Vineyard, Stone Hill Wine Company

Arkansas	Cowie Wine Cellars, Mt Bethel Winery, Wiederkehr Wine Cellars
New Mexico	Anderson Valley Vineyards, Blue Teal Vineyards, La Chiripada Winery, St Clair Vineyards, Sangre de Cristo Wines
Arizona	Sonoita Vineyards, Webb Winery
Montana	Mission Mountain Winery
Idaho	Camas Winery, Petros Winery, Ste Chapelle Winery, Weston

The former Yugoslavia

With the political situation in such confusion, it is best to deal with the wine-growing provinces as we now know them.

Slovenia

The most important white wine-producing province, Slovenia has Ljutomer, Maribor and Ptuz as the commercial centres. Lutomer Riesling is the best-known wine, followed by Lutomer Welschriesling (Laski Riesling) and the sweet Spätlese wine Ranina Radgona (tiger's milk). There is also a small amount of Renski Riesling made using, as the name suggests, the Rhine Riesling grape

Croatia

This is mostly a red wine region with the black Plavac Mali grape widely cultivated. One of the best wines is the full-bodied Dingač made from semi-dried grapes. Other good reds are Postup, Faros, Bolski Plavač and Motovunski Teran. Inland there is a light, straw-coloured wine called Kutjevacka Graševina. Near the Hungarian border in Kontinentalna Hrvatska the Laski Riesling grape makes an abundance of semi-sweet white wines. GRK is a Sherry-style wine made in the island of Korčula.

Bosnia-Herzegovina

This region produces two well-known dry varietal wines. Zilavka is a pungent dry white wine which comes from vineyards around the city of Mostar, and there is a mild-flavoured red wine called Blatina.

Macedonia

Producing mainly red wines from the Vranac and Kratošija grapes, the deep red earthy Kratošija and Teran have the best reputations.

Montenegro

This is also a red wine region with the Vranac grape dominant. The best wine is Crnogorski Vranac.

Serbia

This large region makes red, white and rosé wines. The reds and rosés are made mostly from the Prokupac grape, Smederevka is the principal white grape. The better vineyards are located around Zupa, south of Belgrade, but many of the best white wines come from grapes grown on the cool hillsides of Fruška Gora. German commercial sources have helped Kosova to develop dry to sweetish red wines which sell under the brand name Amselfeld (German for Kosova). Made from the Pinot Noir grape, these wines are extremely popular in Germany and are now beginning to make wine waves in Britain.

6

WINE-BASED DRINKS

Brandy

Brandy is included in this book because it is an extension of wine. Although there are many fruit brandies on the market, strictly speaking brandy is the distillation of wine. The name comes from the Dutch *brandewijn* (burnt wine). Burning was the ancient term used for distilling. Brandy is made in many countries, notably France, Italy, Spain, Germany, Portugal, Australia, USA, South Africa, Greece and Cyprus. Of all the brandies, Cognac, made in the Charente department of France, is best.

Cognac

Cognac is a protected name and the spirit is made from grapes grown in six distinct regions. In descending order of quality these are:

1 Grande Champagne
2 Petite Champagne
3 Borderies
4 Fins Bois
5 Bons Bois
6 Bois Ordinaires and Bois Communs

Although eight species of grapes are allowed by law to be used in the making of Cognac, only three (all white) are in fact used: Saint-Emilion, Folle Blanche and Colombard. They make very ordinary, harsh wine which reveals true greatness only when distilled. The distillation takes place in copper pot stills. When the temperature passes 78°C (172°F), alcoholic vapours rise into a pipe called a swan's neck

COGNAC DISTRICT

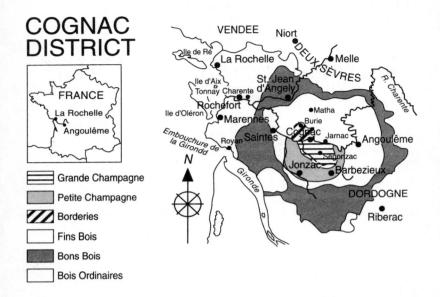

- Grande Champagne
- Petite Champagne
- Borderies
- Fins Bois
- Bons Bois
- Bois Ordinaires

Fig. 6.1 Cognac-producing areas

(because of its shape). This carries the vapours into a condenser where they are changed into a liquid raw spirit. This first distillation is called première chauffe and is made up of:

1 the head (*tête*) – the first part of the liquid to emerge. It is very pungent and unpleasant;
2 the heart (*brouillis*) – the middle and best portion of the distillate. This is taken to one side to be redistilled – it has an alcoholic strength of 30 per cent by volume;
3 the taile (*queue*) – the final liquid to emerge. Besides being very low in alcohol (water vapours have mingled at this stage), it is full of impurities.

The tête and queue are taken aside and later added to any new wine about to be distilled in order to purify them by distillation. The brouillis is now distilled and this second distillation, known as the *bonne chauffe*, is called locally *la vigne en fleur* – the vine in flower. It has an alcoholic strength of 70 per cent by volume and is full of fiery flavour as well as numerous trace elements.

Maturation

The young spirit (bonne chauffe) is put into special wooden casks made of Limousin oak – the wood adds its own character and colour to Cognac. As maturing continues, the spirit is checked from time to time. If the quality is exceptional, it is awarded RN (Reserve Nouvelle) status and put into a section of the cellar known as the *paradise* where all the vintage Cognacs mature to a great age. These are used later to help the quality and style of less-fine products. (It is very unusual to see a bottle of vintage Cognac.)

Quality is helped by ageing in cask – the longer the better – because Cognac, like all spirits, improves only while maturing in cask, it does not improve with age in the bottle. An annual evaporation loss of 3 per cent – known as the 'angels' share' is common and so casks are topped up each year with younger brandy to allow for this.

Brandies of great age and refinement are, of necessity, very expensive and are known as liqueur brandies. They should not be confused with brandy liqueurs which are liqueurs with a brandy base. Age is indicated by stars and words on the label, although these may be interpreted differently by different producers.

Label language

*	3 years maturing in cask
**	4 years in cask
***	5 years in cask
VO	(very old) 10–12 years in cask
VSO	(very superior or special old) 12–17 years in cask
VSOP	(very superior or special old pale) 20–25 years in cask
VVSOP	(very very superior or special old pale) 40 years in cask
XO	up to 45 years in cask
Extra	70 years in cask
Fine Maison	brandy of the house
Fine Champagne	Cognac made from Grande and Petite Champagne grown grapes
Grande Fine Champagne	Cognac made only from Grande Champagne grapes

Popular brands

The following are the brand names most frequently associated with Cognac:

Hennessy	Rémy Martin	Bisquit
Martell	Prince Hubert de Polignac	Courvoisier
Camus	Hine	Otard

Armagnac

From the Gers department to the south-east of Bordeaux comes the world's second best brandy – Armagnac. The grapes Picpoule (Folle Blanche), Saint-Emilion, Jurançon and Colombard make a basic white wine which is produced in three areas: Bas-Armagnac (the best area), Ténarèze and Haut Armagnac. This wine is distilled in a special type of continuous still and aged in black oak barrels for up to 20 years. For real quality look for Grand-Bas-Armagnac or Grand Bas on the label. The best brands are Janneau, Sempé, Marquis de Montesquieu and Marquis de Puységur.

Other well-known brandies

Brandy is made in a variety of different countries – in fact, it can be produced anywhere that wine is made. Below is a list of the most well-known brandies available, other than Cognac and Armagnac. They are usually lower in quality and less expensive than these two brandies.

Asbach Uralt (Germany)
Christian Brothers ⎫
Korbel   ⎬ (USA)
Paul Masson   ⎭
Fundador ⎫
Lepanto   ⎬
Conde de Osborne ⎬ (Spain)
Bobadilla 103 ⎭
Pisco (Chile)

Vecchia Romagna ⎫ (Italy)
Stock   ⎭
Oude Meester (South Africa)
Cambas ⎫ (Greece)
Metaxa ⎭
Anglias   ⎫
Five Kings ⎬ (Cyprus)
Peristiani VO 31 ⎭
Best's St Andrew's (Australia)

The following are brandies made from grape residue pressings which, when fermented and distilled, produce a fiery brandy full of personality that sends searchlights through your body – but oh, the after glow!

Aguardiente (Spain)   Bagaciera (Portugal)
Marc (France)   Grappa (Italy)

Service of brandy

Brandy should be served at room temperature in thin glasses that can be easily warmed in the hand to enhance the bouquet and flavour. There is no need for the gimmicky glass heaters which you see sometimes in 'with it' places. Brandy balloons are the best glasses to use as they curve in narrowly at the top to contain the aroma. Over-large balloons are wasteful, pretentious and make the measure appear stingy. Ginger ale, soda water or 7-Up may be added to brandy, but only the cheaper varieties of spirit should be so adulterated.

—— Aromatised wines and bitters ——

Vermouth

The name vermouth is derived from the German Wermutwein – a wine flavoured with wormwood which, because of its therapeutic and digestive properties, was once highly esteemed as a medicine. Historically the production of vermouth was based in Turin in Italy and Marseille in France. Traditionally, Italy produces the sweet red pungent style and France the light dry white variety. Today there is no such style demarcation as both these and other countries make a variety of vermouths.

Vermouth is made from about 50 different ingredients. These include fruit, roots, barks, peels, flowers, quinine and a variety of herbs. The herbs are specially chosen for their aroma and medicinal properties. The basic wine used is ordinary and placid rather than good. It is matured for about three years and then *mistelle* (unfermented grape juice with the addition of brandy) is added. Meanwhile, the flavouring agents are macerated or infused in alcohol. This flavoured spirit is then added to the wine mixture and the lot is thoroughly blended in large tanks. At this stage some tannin may be added to give more flavour depth. The liquid is then fined, filtered, pasteurised and finally refrigerated to ensure that any remaining tartrates crystallise and fall to the bottom of the tank.

Vermouth must be rested for a short period before being bottled for sale. A short shelf-life is ideal as it does not improve in bottle and is meant to be drunk young.

Vermouth types

There are four main types of vermouth.

Dry vermouth
Often called French vermouth or simply French, it is made from dry white wine that is flavoured and fortified.

Sweet vermouth / Bianco
This is made from dry white wine, flavoured, fortified and sweetened with sugar or mistelle.

Rosé vermouth
Made in a similar way to Bianco, is less sweet and is coloured with caramel.

Red vermouth
Often called Italian vermouth, Italian or more usually It (as in Gin and It), it is made from white wine and is flavoured, sweetened and coloured with a generous addition of caramel.

Popular brands

Cinzano Red	Martini Rosé ⎫	Martini ⎫
Cinzano Bianco	Martini Rosso ⎬ sweet	Cinzano ⎪
Martini Bianco	Noilly Prat Red ⎭	Chambéry ⎬ dry
		Noilly Prat ⎭

The delicate, dryish Chambéryzette is made in the Savoy Alps of France and is flavoured with the juice of wild strawberries. Punt-e-Mes from Carpano of Turin is heavily flavoured with quinine and has wild contrasts of bitterness and sweetness. It is the personality vermouth, people either love it or hate it. Try it on the rocks with a slice of orange. Carpano is a similar style of vermouth but less bitter to the taste.

Service of vermouth

Use a Paris goblet or any stemmed glass. Serve a measure either chilled or with ice, soda water, tonic water or lemonade. It mixes well with sundry spirits and is an important ingredient for many cocktails. A lemon slice is the garnish for the dry varieties and a cherry on a cocktail stick for the sweet styles.

Bitters

Bitters are used either as apéritifs or for flavouring mixed drinks and cocktails. The most popular varieties are mentioned below.

Campari

Campari is most favoured as an apéritif. It has an alcohol strength of 25 per cent by volume and is made from a blend of herbs, gentia, bitter orange peel and quinine all of which have been macerated in spirit. It is rich red-pink in colour and is best served with ice, a slice of orange and topped up with soda water. Many prefer it with tonic water, lemonade, sparkling mineral water or orange juice.

Angostura bitters

Angostura bitters was once made in a town of the same name in Bolivia. The town is now known as Ciudad Bolívar and today Angostura is produced in Trinidad. It is made from gentian and veg-etable spices and is known as the 'Worcester sauce' of the cocktail business. Angostura is an essential ingredient in that famous British naval drink 'Pink Gin' and for the classic 'Champagne Cocktail'.

Byrrh (pronounced beer)

This is a style of bitters made in France near the Spanish border. It has a base of red wine and is flavoured with quinine and herbs and fortified with brandy.

Other well-known bitters are Fernet Branca, Amora Montenegro, Radis, Unicum, Underberg, Abbots, Peychaud, Boonekamp and Welling. Many are used to cure that 'morning after the night before' feeling. Cassis or grenadine are sometimes added to make the drink more palatable. Orange and peach bitters are also essential ingredi-ents for some cocktails.

Other aromatised wines

Dubonnet

Dubonnet is available in two varieties: blonde (white) and rouge (red) and is flavoured with quinine and herbs. It was first made by Joseph Dubonnet as a tonic but modern versions made in South-West France have a wine base with mistelle, spirit and flavouring added.

St Raphaël

This red or white, bitter-sweet drink from France is flavoured with herbs and quinine. It is a style of *ratafia*, once the 'good will' drink offered when a legal document was signed or 'ratified'.

Lillet

Lillet is a very popular French apéritif made from white Bordeaux wine and flavoured with herbs, fruit peels and fortified with Armagnac brandy. It is aged in oak casks.

Pineau des Charentes

Although not strictly an aromatised or fortified wine, Pineau des Charentes has gained popularity as an alternative apéritif or digestif. It is available in white, rosé or red and is made with grape must from the Cognac region and fortified with young Cognac to about 17 per cent alcohol by volume.

—— Wine-based mixed drinks ——

For parties and festive occasions, or for whatever reason, wine-based mixed drinks are hard to beat. They can be cool and refreshing or warm and comforting, but they are always palatable and very enjoyable to drink. They are not difficult to make either, but try to keep to the recipes as the substitution of ingredients often leads to disappointing results. The following drinks have withstood the test of time and changing fashion. They also include some more recent mixes whose popularity has endured sufficiently long to merit classic status. For practicality, we present them under three main styles:

1 Champagne or sparkling wine-based drinks
2 White wine-based drinks
3 Red wine-based drinks

Champagne or sparkling wine-based drinks

Bellini

This Italian drink is made from dry sparkling wine and liquidised peaches.

One third glass chilled peach juice
Champagne or Asti Spumante

Classically it is made by putting the chilled peach juice into a stemmed glass and topping it up with cold Champagne or sparkling wine.

Black Velvet

One half tankard chilled Champagne
One half tankard Guinness
Pour the Champagne and Guinness simultaneously into a chilled silver tankard, taking great care to avoid frothing over.

Buck's Fizz

1 measure chilled, fresh orange juice
1 dash grenadine
chilled Champagne

Stir the orange juice and grenadine together in a wine glass. Top up with Champagne (it should be Bollinger, but other brands can be substituted). Decorate with a slice of orange or a strip of orange peel.

Champagne Cocktail

Champagne
1 sugar lump
Angostura bitters
1 teaspoon Cognac/orange curaçao

Dampen the sugar lump with Angostura and place in a Champagne glass (the saucer style if you prefer). Pour over well chilled

Champagne and float the Cognac or orange curaçao over the back of a teaspoon. Decorate with a slice of orange and a cocktail cherry or, more simply, with a strip of orange peel.

Champagne Cup
(serves 6–8)

2 measures brandy
2 measures curaçao
2 tablespoons caster sugar
1 thinly sliced orange
1 thinly sliced lemon
a few chunks of banana
a few cubes of pineapple
some grapes, strawberries and raspberries
a sprig of borage

Mix all the ingredients together in a glass bowl. Place in fridge for two hours. Just before serving pour over a bottle of ice-cold Champagne.

Doctor Durkan
(serves 6–8)

3 measures Irish Mist
2 measures double cream
1 measure white rum
1 bottle Champagne

Mix the first three ingredients in a glass jug and refrigerate for one hour. Then gradually add the Champagne stirring, at first, to mix. Pour into frosted glasses and decorate with sprigs of mint.

French '75'

1 measure gin
One half measure lemon juice
1 teaspoon caster sugar
ice

Put all the ingredients into a highball glass. Stir well. Top up with cold Champagne.

Kir Royale

1 teaspoon crème de cassis
Champagne

Put the crème de cassis into a Champagne flûte or tulip glass. Top up with cold Champagne.

Mimosa

One third glass chilled fresh orange juice
Two thirds glass cold Champagne
Place the orange juice in a stemmed glass. Top up with cold Champagne.

Note: For economy reasons only, sparkling wine may be used instead of Champagne.

White wine-based drinks

Hock Cup
(serves 6)

One half bottle Rhine wine
2 measures medium sherry
1 measure curaçao
soda water

Pour the wine, sherry and curaçao into a jug. Add ice, top up with soda water and decorate with a slice of lemon and cucumber rind.

Kir

chilled dry white Burgundy (e.g. Chablis or Aligoté)
1 teaspoon crème de cassis

Put the crème de cassis in a goblet and pour over the chilled white wine.

Spritzer

One half glass white wine
soda water or sparkling mineral water

Put the wine and a few ice cubes into a highball glass. Top up with soda water or mineral water and stir gently.

Wine Chiller

One half glass of cold, dry white wine
1 scoop of orange sorbet
One half measure Southern Comfort
Put all the ingredients into a blender. Blend until smooth. Pour into a stemmed glass and drink through a straw.

Wine Cooler

1 small glass red or white wine
4 dashes grenadine
soda water

Place the wine and grenadine in a highball glass. Add ice and top up with soda water.

Red wine-based drinks

Claret Cup
(serves 6–8)

1 bottle claret (red Bordeaux wine)
2 tablespoons sugar
juice 1 orange
juice 1 lemon
2 measures orange curaçao
125 ml (one quarter pint) drinking water
rind of orange and lemon

Boil the sugar and the lemon and orange rinds in the water. Put these into a container along with the claret, curaçao and fruit juices. Stir and leave in the fridge until ready to serve. Put ice into a glass bowl and pour over the Claret Cup. Decorate with very thin slices of cucumber, apple and orange. Ladle into glasses and decorate each glass with a sprig of mint.

Sangria
(serves 12)

1 bottle reasonable quality Spanish red wine
3 measures brandy
125 ml (one quarter pint) orange juice
500 ml (1 pint) lemonade

Pour all the ingredients, together with some ice, into a glass bowl or other glass container. Stir until cold. Decorate with thin slices of orange, lemon and lime.

Mulled wine and winter warmers

Dr Johnson's Choice
(serves 12)

1 bottle claret (red Bordeaux wine)
1 wineglassful orange curaçao
1 wineglassful brandy
sliced orange
12 lumps sugar
6 cloves
500 ml (1 pint) boiling water

Heat the wine with the orange slices, cloves and sugar until nearly boiling. Add the boiling water, curaçao and brandy. Pour into glasses and sprinkle grated nutmeg over the top of each drink.

Mull of Mayo
(serves 20)

2 bottles Burgundy/Rhône red wine
One quarter bottle dark rum
One half bottle Dubonnet
One half bottle drinking water
1 orange liberally studded with cloves
2 cinnamon sticks
25 g (1 oz) sultanas
2 lemon halves
5 g (one quarter oz) mixed spice
1 400 g (1 lb) jar clear honey

Heat the orange in the oven for 10 minutes to bring out the full flavours. Tie the mixed spices securely in a muslin bag to prevent cloudiness, so that only the flavour will be released.

Then place all the ingredients, except the rum, in a large pot – do not use all the honey so the flavour can be adjusted later. Place the pot on a low heat and stir occasionally. Bring the mixture to boiling point, but do not allow to boil. Add the rum, stir, taste and add more honey if necessary. Return to boiling point and then serve into goblets using a ladle with a lip. Sprinkle a little nutmeg over each drink.

Serve immediately while it is fresh and hot. (Tepid mulled wine is insipid.)

The Bishop
(serves 12)

1 and a half bottles ruby port
50 g (2 oz) lump sugar
2 oranges
2 cinnamon sticks
cloves
500 ml (1 pint) water

Prick one of the oranges all over with cloves. Place this in a medium oven for about half an hour.

Pour the port into a saucepan and bring to boiling point, but do not allow to boil. Meanwhile, boil the water with the cinnamon sticks and the baked orange. Rub the sugar lumps against the skin of half of the second orange and place in a serving bowl with the juice of the orange. Combine the heated port and boiling water and pour into the serving bowl. Allow the cinnamon sticks to remain in the bowl, together with the orange 'hedgehog' for decoration.

In the absence of a suitable serving bowl, the mulled wines and winter warmers can be stored in bottles placed in a basin of hot water. When serving, a clean napkin should be wrapped around each bottle.

SOME QUESTIONS
ANSWERED

Q *What do you do if the cork breaks when you are opening the bottle?*

A If the cork breaks but it is still solid in the neck of the bottle, then it may be removed by trying to put the corkscrew back into the cork. To avoid this though, if when removing the cork it starts to break, screw the corkscrew in further before attempting to remove the cork fully. If the cork has broken and attempting to remove the cork merely pushes it into the bottle, then the only course of action is to push it completely into the bottle.

Q *What do you do if the cork goes into the bottle when you are trying to open it?*

A There are two choices: either leave the cork in the bottle and serve the wine, or decant the wine. If you really want to remove the cork then this can be done with a piece of clean string. Loop the string and push it into the bottle so that it goes under the cork. Then pull on the two ends of the string slowly until the loop catches under the bottom of the cork. The cork can then be pulled out. An alternative is to use two pieces of wire (cut from a metal coat-hanger, for example) with about 1cm bent in at the ends. These are pushed into the bottle and then pulled up so that the two bent parts catch underneath the bottom of the cork. There are also commercially available cork extractors based on this principle.

Q *How do they get the cork into the bottle?*

A When wet, cork becomes spongy. Corks for bottles are therefore soaked and then, using a specially made tool, the cork is squeezed to make it thinner than the neck of the bottle and pushed in. Once in the bottle, it expands to seal the bottle.

Q *What are the foils on a wine bottle made from?*

A Traditionally, most are made from lead, which is why it is suggested that the foil should be cut under the second lip, in order to keep the wine away from the foil when pouring. A wide range of other metal and plastic foils is now also used.

Q *Do good glasses really make a difference?*

A Yes. If you are going to enjoy the experience of wine, then good glasses enhance the experience. In general you should invest in the best glasses you can afford. Clear, plain and brilliant glass of a good shape is best; coloured glass interferes with the perception of the colour of the wine. Be wary of over-stylised glassware and always consider what the weight of the wine will do to the stability of the glass when filled. Cut glass can be extremely fine but adds little to the perception of the colour of the wine, with the exception of wines such as port, where, because of the high sugar content, the cut glass enhances the reflections of the myriad of colours in the wine.

Q *Why should you be presented with the cork from a bottle of wine in a restaurant?*

A The cork from a bottle of wine, especially for better wines, will have printed on it confirmation of the content of the bottle. This provides you with further reassurance that the wine is as stated on the bottle label. The other reason is so that you can assure yourself that the cork is healthy and, assuming the cork is fairly soft, that the wine has been stored correctly. If the cork is very dry, it is likely that the wine has not been stored on its side, as it should have been, for some time.

Q *Why is mixing your drinks considered not a wise thing to do?*

A There is the adage of not mixing grape and grain, i.e. not mixing your drinking of wine and wine-based drinks with various spirits and beers, but the main reason for not mixing drinks is the same as not assaulting your system with a barrage of different foods. The body can only take so much alcohol but also reacts to having to cope with an over-indulgent, high volume and wide variety of ingredients in a short space of time. Generally, your system, in making you feel unwell, is trying to tell you of its limits. When it makes you vomit, it is attempting to protect itself, and you, from excess.

Q *Why do some bottles of wine have wire on them?*

A Nowadays this is mainly decorative. It was introduced in Spain as a way of indicating that the label of the wine was the original and had not been tampered with.

Q *Do the names of wines always indicate a particular style?*

A No. Names of varietals (specific grape names) will indicate that the wine is made from that grape but in most countries the percentage does not have to be 100 per cent. There will, therefore, be differences caused by blending with other grapes, as well as the differences caused by all the various factors that affect the quality of the wine, such as location, climate, year, methods of vine cultivation (viticulture) and methods of wine making (viniculture). The style of wines with the classic names of regions, areas or particular vineyards may also vary. This can be as simple as the wine being either white or red but also the degree of sweetness may vary. Again, these wines are affected by the various factors indicated above.

Q *Does opening a bottle of white wine in advance make any difference?*

A Experience suggests that it does. This is for the same reason as it is suggested that red wine should be opened in advance. This is, however, an area of some subjective judgement.

Q *Why do bottles of the same wine occasionally taste different?*

A The taste of wine is affected by so many things: the occasion, the time of day, your mood, the company, the glasses, the temperature, the accompanying food and also what has been consumed before the wine is tasted.

Q *What is the sediment in wine bottles?*

A Some of this is organic matter discarded by the wine as it matures. Most of it comes from two sources which is true for both red and white wines. These are the tartrates of calcium and sodium formed by a combination of tartaric acid, which is natural in the wine, and calcium and sodium The sediment only appears different because of the red or white colour of the wine. In some white wines the sediment is often mistaken for sugar crystals but sugar as a natural ingredient of wine, does not form crystals.

Q *Are the smell and taste associations people have of wine the same for everyone?*

A No. Be reassured that the associations people give to smell and taste while often similar are nevertheless individual perceptions. The associations you attach are those that mean something to you.

Q *Is smoking bad for wine tasting?*

A Certainly there should be no smoking in wine-tasting rooms, in the same way as there should be no other aromas around. However, if you do smoke then your perception of the smell and taste of the wine is, and will have been, affected by nicotine being present. When you stop smoking, your perceptions of the smell and taste of wine will change, as will the smell and taste of everything else.

Q *When drinking wine should it be guzzled or sipped?*

A Try taking individual mouthfuls. The sensation will be the same for each mouthful as it will be from guzzling a whole glass. Slow the experience down and enjoy it! Sipping is too slow and doesn't provide sufficient opportunity to savour the wine.

Q *Should water be drunk at meals with wine?*

A Yes. The water quenches the thirst rather than expecting the wine to do it and therefore allows the wine to be enjoyed. Tap or mineral water is fine, but chill mineral water rather than serving it with ice made from tap water. Also avoid lemon with it, as this can affect the taste of the wine.

Q *Why do you seem to be intoxicated by some drinks more quickly than others?*

A Alcohol in sparkling drinks gets to the bloodstream more quickly than in still drinks. Fortified wines come next as they are a mixture of wine and spirit and have a fairly high alcoholic content (14 to 20 per cent by volume). Pure spirits take longer, but then this also means that the body will take longer to deal with the alcohol. Be wary the morning after drinking heavily: you may still be over the legal limit for driving.

Q *How long does table wine keep once the bottle is opened?*

A Wine is at its best when first opened. Light wines deteriorate more quickly than wines with a good alcohol content. The speed of deterioration will also depend on how much wine is left in the bottle – the less wine, the more air and the quicker the wine will spoil. If you use a good stopper, wine will last for a day or two, with the younger, more robust wines having a better chance of survival than the older, more delicate wines. The bottle should be kept in the fridge or in a cool place. There are, of course, wine-preserving gadgets, such as the Vacu-vin, commercially available which will keep the wine healthy for a few days. Fortified wines, such as port and sherry, will keep in reasonable condition for two to three weeks after being opened.

Q *What is organic wine?*

A Organic wine is made from grapes grown by traditional agricultural methods, fertilised with natural materials only and naturally protected from pests and diseases.

Q *Is more expensive wine better value?*

A Since the days of King Alfred, excise duty has had to be paid on wines and spirits in Britain. Each bottle of wine sold attracts the same rate of duty whether the wine is cheap or expensive. Therefore the duty on cheaper wine forms a higher proportion of the total price. So, more expensive wine should be better value.

Q *Do all wines improve as they get older?*

A Not necessarily. Wines sold without a vintage year are usually best drunk soon after purchase. Vintage wines generally continue to improve with age but this does vary. It is best to check vintage charts for drinking or keeping recommendations.

Q *Does tapping a bottle of sparkling wine with a knife or spoon before opening prevent it from frothing over when being opened?*

A We think it does, but for the best result, chill the wine well and do not agitate the bottle before or during the opening process.

Q *When ordering wine to accompany a meal in a restaurant, how much do you allow per person?*

A Allow a half bottle, three glasses, per person.

Q *How do you keep the fizz in sparkling wine once the bottle is opened?*

A There are inexpensive purpose-made stoppers on the market which are efficient in preserving the effervescence. Some people suggest that placing a teaspoon in the neck of the bottle will also keep the bubbles. However, with cheaper sparkling wines the fizz is short-lasting, whatever you try to do.

Q *Can condition of glasses affect the taste of wine?*

A Yes. All glasses have to be kept in prime condition – which means they should be odour-free, dust-free, detergent-free and chip-free. In other words, brilliantly clean. To achieve this, glasses should be rinsed in clean hot water (without detergent) after washing and then dried and polished using absolutely clean, fresh glass-cloths. Glasses should be stored upright so that they do not trap stale air, and preferably in a closed cupboard to keep dust at bay.

Q *Does decanting improve the flavour of red wine?*

A The real purpose of decanting is to separate the wine from its sediment. Decanting also allows the wine to breathe and to develop its bouquet. It also softens the flavour of the wine, which can be interpreted as 'improvement'.

Q *What kind of wine do you use in cooking?*

A The colour of the wine is more important than the quality, but the popular opinion is that the better the wine, the better the sauce. The traditional trend is to use the wine that is to accompany the food at the table in the preparation of the dish.

Q *If you have to choose one wine to accompany the complete meal, what colour should it be?*

A This is a difficult one because so much depends on the main course and on personal preference. However, white and rosé wines are much more versatile than red wines. We think a good rosé wine would be the best compromise, or why not try Champagne?

GLOSSARY OF WINE TERMS

acidity   a number of organic acids are naturally present in grapes, the principal acids being tartaric and malic. Acid imparts lasting qualities to wine and contributes to bouquet and flavour: too much acidity makes wine sharp or sour – mouth puckering – too little results in flat and flabby wine

adegas   Portuguese warehouse for storing and maturing wine

ageing   refers to the maturing of wine in barrel and bottle; ageing imparts mellowness to wine but it must not be overdone, otherwise the wine will lose its fruit flavour

alcohol (ethyl) C_2H_5OH, obtained by the action of yeast on sugar during fermentation; its strength can be further increased by distillation

alcohol content   the alcohol content of wine is expressed as a percentage of the total; most table wines have a strength of between 8 per cent and 15 per cent

American Viticultural Area (AVA)   this appellation system was introduced by the US Bureau of Alcohol, Tobacco and Firearms in the 1980s; the wine regions are officially designated but no quality standard is guaranteed

ampelographer   an expert on grape vines and their behaviour in the vineyard

Añada   a vintage wine in Spain

Appellation contrôlée   French law which guarantees the origin of the wine named on the label (also called Appellation d'Origine Contrôlée)

aroma   the smell of a wine. There are three levels of aroma: varietal aroma, the fresh, fruity smell of grapes; aroma from fermentation; aroma which develops as the wine ages and matures, also known as bouquet

aromatised wines   these, usually fortified wines, are either lightly or heavily flavoured with aromatic substances; vermouth is an example

aspect   the direction a vineyard faces in relation to the sun

assemblage   a French term for the blending of basic wines in order to achieve a balanced end product

atmosphere   applied especially to sparkling wine, it is a measure of atmospheric pressure; 1 atmosphere is equal to 15 pounds per square inch (metric conversion 101,325 N/m^2). A Champagne bottle usually has an internal pressure of six atmospheres

Auslese   German and Austrian style of wine made from late-gathered, specially selected, bunches of ripe grapes

Bag-in-the-Box   an airtight bag usually holding three or ten litres of wine, the bag is made of layers of impermeable plastic enclosed in a cardboard box from which a tap obtrudes allowing access to the wine; synonymous with certain Australian wines

barrique   a barrel or small wooden cask used for ageing wine; it holds 225 litres which will produce 288 bottles of wine

baumé   a scale of measurement to indicate the sugar content in must

Beerenauslese   German or Austrian style of wine made from individually selected overripe single grapes

beeswing   floating sediment that has not settled with the crust in vintage port

bentonite   a special, fine clay which is often used as a fining agent to clear wine

Bereich   a German wine district

bin   slot for holding a bottle of wine in a cellar

Blackstrap   used long ago to describe a rough variety of port; elderberry colouring was usually added to disguise faults

Black Velvet   a mixture of chilled Champagne and Guinness; sometimes called 'Bismark'

blanc de blancs   white wine from white grapes

blanc de noirs   white wine from black grapes

blush wine   pale pinky blue wine from black grapes

bocksbeutel (boxbeutel)   attractive flagon-shaped bottle for holding the Steinwein of Franconia; now used extensively in Portugal

BOB Buyers Own Brand   wine or spirit made to be sold under the name of restaurant or supermarket

bodega   Spanish cellar, warehouse or bar

body   description of strength and fullness in wine

bois   wood – Gout de Bois – woody taste

bonded   wines and spirits are bonded and kept in a warehouse under government supervision until the Customs and Excise duties are paid by the purchaser

Botrytis cinerea   also known as pourriture noble or noble rot. When conditions are right the grapes are attacked by a fungus which shrivels the grapes and concentrates the sugar to produce luscious wines (e.g. Sauternes)

bottle   standard size holds 75 cl

bottle sickness   sometimes happens to newly bottled wines; disappears after some months

boutique winery   a term used in America and Australia to describe a small winery that concentrates essentially on the making of quality wines

breed   name used to describe fine quality wine

brut or nature   driest Champagne; generally no sweetness added

cap   the mass of skins, stalks and pips that rises to the top of the must during fermentation

carbon dioxide CO_2 gas which is one of the by-products of fermentation

carbonic maceration   a style of wine making associated with certain wines such as Beaujolais Nouveau and the Italian-style Vino Novello; whole grapes are put into sealed vats under a blanket of carbonic gas. Natural fermentation takes place inside the grapes which eventually split under their own weight; colour and fruit flavour is extracted but not tannin so the wine is ready to be drunk early, in weeks rather than months

cava   a cellar, also a Spanish term to indicate that sparkling wine is made by the classical method – metodo tradicional

caviste   cellar worker

cellar   below ground storage area

cep   vine stock

cépage   vine variety

chai   above ground storage area

chambrer   to bring wines (usually red) to room temperature

chaptalisation   addition of sugar to grape must to secure higher alcoholic content; amount is strictly controlled by law

charnu   a full-bodied wine

château   castle; also means a wine from a particular vineyard

château bottled   Mise en bouteille au château – signifies that the wine has been bottled at the château, which in itself is a guarantee of quality

chlorosis   a vine disease caused by an imbalance of minerals

claret   English name for the red wines of Bordeaux; comes from the French *clairet* meaning clear, bright, light

climat   vineyard or single plot within a large vineyard

clone   this is a strain of a particular grape species, for example, the classic Riesling grape has many clones

clos   walled vineyard, especially in Burgundy

cobblers   American drink for warm weather; made from wine or spirits, fresh fruit and ice shavings

corkage   a nominal fee that some restaurants charge when they allow customers to bring in their own wine

corked   describes a wine that has been affected by a faulty or diseased cork; it smells awful and tastes as it smells

côtes   hills where some vineyards are located

coulure   too much rain and soil deficiency is the principal cause; the berries on the vine will not develop and stay stunted

coupage   vatting or blending of wine

crémant   creaming, sparkling, effervescent

criadera   nursery for young sherries

cru   growth; also wines of a similar standard

crust   deposit which has gathered especially in bottles of vintage port

cultivar   a term used in South Africa for a grape variety

cuvaison   associated with red wine production when the juice is kept in contact with the skins

cuve   a French vat or cask

cuve close   the bulk method for producing sparkling wine in a closed tank

cuvée   contents of a vat or a blend of wine in the making of Champagne

Denominación de Origen (DO)   Spanish equivalent to AOC of France

Denominación de Origen Calificada (DOC)   the highest classification for Spanish quality wines

Denominazione di Origine Controllata (DOC)   Italian equivalent to DO of Spain and AOC of France

Denominazione di Origine Controllata e Garantita (DOCG) the highest and newest classification of Italian wines

domaine   a single vineyard in France

dosage   addition of sugar dissolved in wine to produce varying degrees of sweetness in sparkling wines

doux   sweet, also dulce

Eiswein   an intensely sweet wine made from frozen grapes in Germany, Austria and Canada

eleveur   the person who 'brings up' the wine and takes care of it until it is ready for sale

en primeur   wine sold within a year of the harvest and before it is bottled

esters   the combination of acids and alcohol which gives wine its bouquet

filtering   the removal of dead yeast, solids and impurities from wine and beer to make them bright in appearance

Fine Champagne   finest Cognac brandy

Fine Maison   brandy of the house

fining   the clearing of wine in cask or tank; fining agents include Isinglass (the bladder of the sturgeon) and egg whites

fusel oil   toxic alcohol (not ethanol) found in spirits as a by-product of distillation

gyropalette   used in the Champagne making remuage process. These computer-controlled, hydrolically operated machines shake the sediment down into the neck of the bottle in preparation for the wine to be cleared by disgorging

hydrometer   an instrument that records the density of alcohol in a wine or spirit

irrigation   artificial means of watering vineyards

laying down   storing of wine in bottle

lees   the sediment that falls to the bottom of the vessel when fermentation is completed

macération carbonique   *see* carbonic maceration

maderised   a term used when a white wine oxidises badly and turns amber in colour, like Madeira wine, hence the name; this may be due to excessive age or, more likely, to bad storage conditions

magnum   bottle size, equivalent to two standard bottles

malo-lactic fermentation   the lactic bacteria convert the harsh malic acid into softer malic acid; there is no increase in alcohol as a result of this secondary fermentation

mousse   French term to describe the froth or bubbles in sparkling wine

mulled wine   heated wine flavoured with spices; in Germany it is called Glüwein

must   unfermented grape juice

négociant   wine handler or merchant or shipper

Öechsle   German system for calculating the specific gravity or must weight in order to estimate the potential alcohol of the grape juice

oenology   the science of wine making

oenophile   a connoisseur of wine

organic wines   wine produced from grapes which have been grown without the use of pesticides, herbicides or chemical fertilisers

Passe-tout-grains   a Burgundy blend of one-third Pinot Noir and two-thirds Gamay for making red wine

Pasteur, Louis   French scientist renowned for his work on fermentation and pasteurisation

pétillant   semi-sparkling

photosynthesis   this happens when the vine, using light energy absorbed by the green chlorophyll of its leaves, converts carbon dioxide and water into usable organic compounds such as carbohydrates

Phylloxera vastatrix   an aphid that feeds on the roots of the vine and kills it; the cure is to graft the European Vitis vinifera on to American rootstock immune to the disease

pruning   the removal of unwanted parts of the vine in order to regulate yield and quality; it is carried out in winter and spring

punt   the dip in the bottom of a bottle; it strengthens and reinforces the bottle and, in the case of Champagne bottles, it stabilises the sediment after fermentation

racking   moving wine from one cask or container into another for the purpose of clearing the wine off its sediment

refractometer   a hand-held instrument or optical device used to gauge the sugar content within the grapes while they are still on the vine; it helps to assess when the grapes are ready for gathering

residual sugar   natural sugar left in wine after fermentation

rince cochon (pigswill)   using red Beaujolais instead of Aligoté as a base for Kir

saccharometer   an instrument for measuring the sugar content in must or wine

Saccharomyces ellipsoideus   the most important wine yeast

sommelier   a wine waiter or wine butler

Süssreserve   unfermented, sterile, grape juice added to give balance and sweetness to some wines before bottling

tannin   astringent acid imparted by stalks, pips and skins in the making of red wines, noticeable by a gum-drying sensation on the palate; it helps to preserve wine as it matures

tastevin   dimpled silver cup used by sommeliers to taste wine

tears   streaks or legs of wine that form on the inside of a glass as the wine is being drunk; they are an indication of a high alcohol and/or glycerine content

vendange   the vintage or harvesting of the grapes

vinification   the making of wine

vintage wine   wine made in a good year

viscosity   when a wine is rolled around a glass, sometimes tears or legs form near the top of the glass and run back down into the wine; this indicates an unctuous, oily wine with a high level of alcohol and sugar

viticulture   the cultivation of the vine

Vitis   the vine genus

Vitis vinifera   wine-bearing vine; the species responsible for all the great wines produced

wash   a fermented liquid destined to be distilled

weeper   wine that is weeping or leaking because of a faulty or dry cork

yeast   uni-cellular fungi found on the skins of grapes; these microorganisms produce zymase, the enzyme which converts sugar into alcohol

yeast autolysis   dead yeast cells which fall to the bottom of a tank or bottle in the production of sparkling wines; it gives the wine a pleasing yeasty, biscuity bouquet

FURTHER READING

Anderson, B. *Wines of Italy*, London, Italian Trade Centre, 1992

Burroughs, D. and Bezzant, N. *The New Wine Companion*, London, Heinemann, 1987

Clarke, O. *The Essential Wine Book*, London, Viking Penguin, 1985

Doxat, J. *Drinks and Drinking*, London, Ward Lock, 1971

Dunkling, L. *The Guinness Drinking Companion*, London, Guinness Publishing, 1992

Durkan, A. *Vendange*, London, Edward Arnold, 1971

Durkan, A. and Cousins, J. *The Beverage Book*, London, Hodder & Stoughton, 1995

Ensrud, B. *American Vineyards*, New York, Stewart, Tabori & Chang, 1988

Foulkes, C. (ed.) *Larousse Encyclopedia Of Wine*, Paris, Larousse, 1994

George, R. *The Wine Dictionary*, London, Longman, 1989

Hogg, A. *Everybody's Wine Guide*, London, Quiller Press, 1985

Jefford, A. *Port*, London, Merehurst Press, 1988

Lillicrap, D. and Cousins, J. *Food and Beverage Service*, 4th edn, London, Hodder & Stoughton, 1994

Prial, F. (ed.) *The Companion to Wine*, London, Mirabel Books, 1992

Stevenson, T. *World Wine Encyclopedia*, London, Dorling Kindersley, 1994

Young, R. *The Really Useful Wine Guide*, London, Sidgwick and Jackson, 1987

INDEX